101 Best Start-Up Business Ideas For 2024 According To Advanced A.I.

Jaime Gehly

Copyright © 2023 Jaime Gehly

All rights reserved.

ISBN: 9798399812687

101 BEST START-UP BUSINESS IDEAS FOR 2024 ACCORDING TO ADVANCED A.I.

101 BEST START-UP BUSINESS IDEAS FOR 2024 ACCORDING TO ADVANCED A.I.

Introduction

As we approach the year 2024, the entrepreneurial landscape is evolving at an unprecedented speed. The fusion of advanced technologies and innovative thinking has paved the way for a new age of start-up business ideas that cater to various niches and industries. Entrepreneurs, now more than ever, have an opportunity to create groundbreaking companies that have the potential to change the world. To help you navigate the exciting world of start-ups, we've compiled a list of the 101 best start-up business ideas for 2024, as predicted by advanced AI.

The list features an array of industries that are ripe for disruption, including healthcare, education, transportation, and sustainability. For instance, AI-driven telehealth platforms that provide remote medical consultations and personalized treatment plans are expected to gain immense traction in the coming years. Similarly, education start-ups with a focus on immersive learning experiences through virtual reality and adaptive learning technologies offer promising opportunities for entrepreneurs.

Another booming sector is sustainable transportation solutions. As urban populations continue to grow and environmental concerns take center stage, entrepreneurs who can develop novel approaches to transportation, such as autonomous vehicles or electric bikes, will find themselves at the forefront of this industry. Additionally, innovative business models in the sharing economy, such as shared workspaces and co-living spaces, will continue to gain popularity as people seek more affordable and flexible options for living and working in urban environments.

The AI's predictions also highlight the potential for start-ups focusing on mental health and well-being. With stress and anxiety becoming increasingly prevalent in modern society, there is a growing demand for services that help individuals manage their mental health effectively. Entrepreneurs who can develop accessible digital tools or platforms that cater to this need are likely to find great success in this emerging market.

These start-up business ideas for 2024 present a diverse range of opportunities for aspiring entrepreneurs. May the following pages help guide you towards your next greatest success!

JAIME GEHLY

CONTENTS

Technology and Innovation

1. Blockchain-Based Voting System 2
2. VR/AR-Based Fitness Application 4
3. Online Education and Tutoring 6
4. RFID-Based Inventory Management 8
5. 3D Printing Niche Products 10
6. E-Commerce Automation Tools 12
7. Subscription Box Services 14
8. AI-Based Language Learning Software 16
9. Robotics Kits and Tutorials for Kids 18
10. IoT-Based Agricultural Monitoring Solutions 20
11. Smart Kitchen Appliances 22
12. AI-Driven Virtual Event Platforms 24
13. Chatbot-Based E-Commerce 26
14. Voice Command Applications 28
15. VR/AR-Based Escape Rooms 30
16. Blockchain-Based Supply Chain Management 32
17. VR-Based Travel Experiences 34
18. IoT-Based Home Automation Systems 36
19. QR-Code Based Contactless Payments 38
20. Cybersecurity Services for Small Businesses 40
21. AI-Driven Biotech Research 42
22. Live Streaming Platforms and Tools 44
23. AI-Based Emotion Recognition Technology 46
24. Smart Home Security Consultancy 48
25. Robotics For Agricultural Use 50
26. Streamlined Home Renovation Solutions 52
27. Privacy-Focused Messaging Apps and Services 54
28. Voice Assistant Integration Services 56

Lifestyle, Education, and Entertainment

29. AI-Generated Personalized Fashion 60
30. Eco-Friendly Fashion Retail 62
31. Drone-Based Delivery Services 64
32. Premium Pet Care Services 66
33. Micro-Mobility Solutions 68
34. Personal Finance Management Apps 70
35. Travel Planning and Booking Platform 72
36. Online Maker Spaces for Craftsmen 74
37. Adaptive E-Learning Platforms 76
38. Socially-Conscious Artisan Marketplaces 78
39. Ethical Cosmetics: Cruelty-Free and Eco-Friendly 80
40. Esports Coaching Platforms 82
41. Plant-Based Meat Alternatives 84
42. Remote Team Collaboration Tools 86
43. Sleep Optimization Solutions 88
44. Space Tourism 90
45. Lab-Grown Meat Production 92
46. Minimalist Living and Lifestyle Consulting 94
47. Gamified E-Learning Apps 96
48. Locavore Meal-Kit Delivery Services 98
49. Hyper-Local News Apps 100
50. Electric Vehicle Charging Stations 102
51. Smart Eldercare Solutions 104
52. On-Demand House Cleaning Services 106
53. Coworking Space Management Solutions 108
54. Virtual Coworking Spaces 110
55. Content Personalization Services 112
56. Micro-Investing/Stocks Trading Platforms 114

57. Home-Schooling Tools and Resources 116
58. AI-Driven Content Marketing Tools 118
59. Location And Activity-Based Social Networks 120
60. Personalized Learning AI for Kids 122
61. Disaster Management and Risk Prediction Tools 124
62. Virtual Reality Art Galleries 126
63. AI-Generated Music and Art Platforms 128
64. Gig Economy Job Platforms 130

Healthcare, Wellness, and Fitness

65. AI-Driven Healthcare Services 134
66. Personalized Nutrition Platforms 136
67. Mental Health Chatbot Services 138
68. Telemedicine Platforms 140
69. Mental Wellness Apps 142
70. Art Therapy Platforms 144
71. Adaptive Therapy Management 146
72. DNA-Based Skincare and Wellness Solutions 148
73. Neurotech Solutions 150
74. Personalized Genomics and Medicine 152
75. Smart Fitness Wearables 154
76. Mental Health Tracking and Support Platform 156
77. Wearable Health Monitoring Devices 158
78. Nutrition And Fitness App Integrations 160
79. Community-Driven Wellness Platforms 162

Sustainability and Environment

80. Sustainable Packaging Solutions 166
81. Renewable Energy Solutions 168
82. Green Transport Methods 170
83. Smart Waste Management Solutions 172
84. Energy Storage Solutions 174
85. Circular Economy Marketplaces 176
86. Carbon Capture and Storage Solutions 178
87. Sustainable Event Planning 180
88. Carbon Offset Marketplace 182
89. Sustainable Fashion Resale Platforms 184
90. Hydroponic Home Garden Systems 186
91. Smart City Infrastructure Solutions 188
92. Peer-To-Peer Electricity Grid 190
93. Smart Water Management Systems 192
94. Vertical Aeroponic Farming 194
95. Sustainable Product Innovations 196
96. Zero-Waste Product Stores 198
97. Native Plant Landscaping Services 200
98. AI-Driven Climate Change Solutions 202
99. Smart Urban Farming Solutions 204

Ethical and Social Impact

100. AI-Based Talent Acquisition Platforms 208
101. Ethical AI Consultation and Implementation Services 210

The Future of IoT

A Success Story from the Lighting Industry 214

Technology And Innovation

Blockchain-Based Voting System

Establishing a blockchain-based voting system start-up will be a wise and profitable investment, owing to the growing need for safe and efficient voting procedures. Blockchain technology enables a tamper-proof, transparent, and secure system that contributes significantly to the essence of democracy. To launch a successful start-up, the process should involve market research, a comprehensive business plan, regulatory compliance, team building, and securing funding.

Blockchain technology, the innovative cryptographic system that underpins cryptocurrencies like Bitcoin, provides an excellent framework for a voting platform. In future years, demand for secure voting solutions will continue to rise, as traditional voting procedures have demonstrated their weaknesses in terms of transparency and integrity. A blockchain-based voting system start-up has the potential to revolutionize the democratic process and attract global customers, leading to substantial financial and societal success.

Advantages of a Blockchain-based Voting System:

1. **Security**: Blockchain technology ensures data immutability and decentralization, creating a tamper-proof environment for voting data storage. This attribute guarantees that votes cannot be erased, altered, or interfered with, maintaining the integrity of the election process.

2. **Transparency and Auditability**: Blockchain-based voting systems offer an unparalleled level of transparency, enabling stakeholders to verify and audit election results with ease. This fosters trust in the electoral process and ensures that all parties involved have access to accurate, reliable data.

3. **Accessibility**: A blockchain-based voting system start-up allows for remote accessibility, enabling secure electronic voting for individuals with disabilities, military personnel stationed overseas, and citizens living abroad. The online voting mechanism encourages participation and streamlines the voting process.

Steps to Launch a Blockchain-Based Voting System Start-up:

1. **Market Research**: A thorough examination of existing voting systems and successful use cases will provide insights into the needs of potential customers, as well as the strengths and weaknesses of competitors. This information will guide the development of a unique value proposition for the start-up.

2. **Comprehensive Business Plan**: A well-structured business plan will outline the goals and strategies required to develop the platform. Considerations should include the technical aspects, market positioning, business model, go-to-market strategy, and operations.

3. **Regulatory Compliance**: Regulations surrounding the application of blockchain technology to voting systems will vary by location. Engage with legal experts to navigate the relevant regulatory landscape, ensuring the proper licenses and permissions are obtained to operate on a local, national, or global level.

4. **Team Building and Partnerships**: Assemble a team with expertise in computer science, blockchain technology, cybersecurity, and User Experience (UX) design. Collaborate with election organizers and governments to understand requirements and ensure platform adoption.

5. **Secure Funding**: Acquire financial support through various channels, such as crowdfunding, angel investors, venture capital, or government grants. Early, transparent communication and demonstrations of market potential will facilitate investor confidence and secure the funding needed for success.

In conclusion, launching a blockchain-based voting system start-up in 2024 has immense potential for both societal impact and financial success. By addressing transparency, security, and accessibility issues, this innovative venture will revolutionize the democratic process and empower citizens across the globe. A carefully planned and executed strategy is the foundation for the success of such an ambitious project.

VR/AR-Based Fitness Applications

A VR/AR-based fitness application start-up is predicted to be a successful venture, given the accelerated market dynamics, digital transformation of society, and an increased focus on health and wellness. By following basic steps such as market research, product development, funding, and marketing strategies, a viable start-up can be established in this domain.

As the world reaches 2024, the market for virtual reality (VR) and augmented reality (AR) technologies have significantly evolved, expanding their reach and integration into various industries. Continuous advancements in technology and a growing preference for virtual solutions have created a ripe environment for a VR/AR-based fitness application start-up.

Market Potential:

The global VR/AR market is expected to witness tremendous growth, with estimates reaching USD 296.9 billion by 2024. The fitness industry, already a multibillion-dollar market, is experiencing increased demand for personalized, smart, and interactive fitness solutions, fueled in part by the ongoing COVID-19 pandemic. Combining these factors indicates that a VR/AR fitness application start-up has considerable potential for success in 2024.

Consumer Preferences:

The increasing inclination toward home-based fitness and remote training is pushing consumers to seek innovative solutions for engaging and entertaining workout experiences. VR and AR technologies provide an immersive and gamified approach to fitness, which caters to the evolving preferences of consumers worldwide.

Steps to Start a VR/AR Fitness Application Business:

1. **Market Research**: Perform comprehensive market research to gain insights into the industry, target audience preferences, and potential competitors. Analyze existing solutions, market gaps, and opportunities for innovation. Identify potential obstacles and prepare strategies to overcome them.

2. **Product Development**: Capture the unique value proposition for the start-up and design a VR/AR fitness application that satisfies market needs. Plan and create high-quality content, with user-friendly interfaces and robust functionalities. Consult fitness professionals, UX/UI designers, and VR/AR developers to ensure that the application is tailored to user needs and accessible fitness levels.

3. **Funding**: Explore funding options such as angel investments, venture capital, crowdfunding, or government grants, and secure the necessary capital for product development, marketing, and operational costs. Prepare a solid business plan and financial projections to attract potential investors.

4. **Marketing Strategies**: Design a comprehensive marketing plan to create awareness, engage the target audience, and acquire users. Embrace digital marketing tools such as social media, content marketing, influencer partnerships, and PR for promoting the application. Consider offering free trials, limited-time promotions, or other incentives to gain early traction.

5. **Launch and Continuous Improvement**: After developing and extensively testing the application, launch it on relevant platforms. Collect user feedback, monitor usage data, and continuously iterate to improve the quality, performance, and customer satisfaction of the application. Stay up-to-date on industry trends and technological advancements, refining the product as necessary to remain competitive.

A VR/AR-based fitness application start-up has all the ingredients for success in 2024, given the strong market interest, a growing worldwide focus on health and wellness, and flexible technology development options.

Online Education and Tutoring

The emergence of technological advancements and evolving educational needs will make the online education and tutoring startup business a lucrative venture. The world has seen a significant shift towards flexible and accessible learning solutions, with learners and parents preferring personalized and on-demand education. By properly understanding the audience and executing the right strategies, a start-up in online education and tutoring can thrive in the competitive market of 2024.

Factors Contributing to the Success:

1. **Growing Demand for Online Learning**: The global pandemic has accelerated the adoption of online and remote learning, making it a fundamental component of education. This trend will continue to grow even after the pandemic, as people become more accustomed to the convenience and accessibility of online learning.

2. **Technological Advancements**: In 2024, cutting-edge technologies like Artificial Intelligence, Virtual Reality, and Augmented Reality will expand the scope of online education, making it more interactive, immersive, and personalized.

3. **Increasing Access to the Internet**: The expansion of the internet to remote areas will further contribute to the demand for online education and tutoring services.

4. **Flexible and Personalized Education**: Online tutoring allows students to get personalized learning experiences according to their learning styles, strengths, and weaknesses. This specialized attention helps students maximize their potential while accommodating their busy schedules.

5. **Cost-Effective Alternatives**: Online education and tutoring services can offer more affordable solutions when compared to traditional institutions, making quality education accessible to a larger population.

Basic Steps to Launch an Online Education and Tutoring Start-up Business:

1. **Market Research**: Start with thorough market research to identify the target audience, possible niches, and competitors in the online education landscape. This will help in developing an effective business plan.

2. **Develop a Business Plan**: Create a comprehensive business plan outlining the mission, marketing strategies, revenue model, operational costs, and projected growth. This will act as a roadmap to drive the direction and decisions for the start-up.

3. **Choose the Appropriate Technology**: Select the right Learning Management System (LMS) and other essential tools to deliver online tutoring and courses efficiently. Leverage technological advancements, such as AI-based learning and analytics systems, to provide an engaging learning experience.

4. **Create High-Quality Content**: Develop engaging, relevant, and interactive course materials that align with the curriculum guidelines and cater to the target audience's needs. Collaborate with experts or subject matter specialists to ensure content accuracy and effectiveness.

5. **Legality and Compliance**: Obtain necessary licenses and permits, and adhere to the regulatory requirements for running an online education and tutoring start-up. Ensure data privacy and student safety by implementing secure systems and guidelines.

6. **Marketing and Promotion**: Develop a strategic marketing plan to create brand awareness and reach the target audience. Utilize social media, educational websites, partnerships, and content marketing to expand the potential customer base.

7. **Continuously Evaluate and Adapt**: Track the performance of the business regularly and revise strategies accordingly. Adapt to new trends in the education sector and update the platform and content to remain relevant and competitive.

RFID-Based Inventory Management

An RFID-based inventory management start-up can witness widespread success and high profitability. The core value propositions include increased efficiency, improved data accuracy, streamlined processes, reduction in losses, and enhanced decision-making capabilities. This summary covers the foundational benefits of an RFID-based inventory management start-up and outlines the basic steps required to build a successful venture in 2024.

Market Opportunity:

1. **Increased Demand for Automation**: With businesses rapidly expanding and requiring intelligent systems to manage their supply chains, the demand for RFID-based inventory management solutions will continue to grow. Start-ups offering specialized and customized RFID solutions cater to diverse industries like retail, logistics, manufacturing, automotive, and healthcare.

2. **Improved Technology**: The constant advancements in RFID technology, with smaller, faster, and more cost-effective tags, give start-ups the ideal window to create solutions with high accuracy that seamlessly integrate into existing business processes.

3. **Technological Integration**: RFID-based inventory management systems can be easily integrated with other technologies like IoT, big data analytics, and AI, creating holistic supply chain management platforms.

Key Benefits of RFID-Based Inventory Management Systems:

1. **Efficiency**: Automation of inventory tracking using RFID reduces time spent on manual inventory counting, locating items, and managing stock, resulting in higher productivity.

2. **Accuracy**: RFID technology minimizes human errors in data entry by automatically scanning and updating inventory data, thereby improving overall data quality.

3. **Inventory Optimization**: Real-time visibility into inventory levels and location enables businesses to optimize stock levels, effectively reducing carrying costs and stockouts.

4. **Loss Prevention**: RFID inventory management systems provide businesses with enhanced security and loss prevention capabilities by monitoring and identifying potential product theft or misplacement.

5. **Decision-making**: Accurate, real-time data allows organizations to make better-informed, data-driven decisions on inventory management, demand forecasting, and resource allocation.

Starting an RFID-Based Inventory Management Start-up:

1. **Market Research**: Conduct a comprehensive market analysis to understand the target industries, potential clients, and competitors in the RFID integrated solutions space, identifying specific needs and pain-points that your start-up can resolve.

2. **Product Development**: Design and develop a market-ready RFID-based inventory management solution, focusing on user-friendliness, customization, scalability, and integration with other technological platforms. Seek expert input to optimize software and component selections.

3. **Pilot and Testing**: Before commercializing the product, test its efficiency, accuracy, and real-world functionality across various scenarios, collecting user feedback to iterate and fine-tune the offering.

4. **Regulatory Compliance**: Ensure regulatory compliance with intellectual property, data privacy, and specific industry regulations as applicable to the product and target market.

5. **Marketing and Sales**: Develop a go-to-market strategy by identifying target customers, choosing effective communication channels, and implementing sales methodologies to generate leads, educate potential clients, and close deals.

6. **Support and Maintenance**: Establish a robust customer support and maintenance infrastructure to troubleshoot issues, provide software updates, and develop long-term client relationships.

Embracing the opportunities presented in 2024, an RFID-based inventory management start-up shows promising potential for success and high profitability with the right approach. By targeting specific market needs, exploiting technological advancements, and showcasing the efficiency and accuracy benefits of RFID-based inventory management, new ventures can tap into this booming market segment.

3D Printing Niche Products

A 3D printing niche products startup would undoubtedly be a highly successful and profitable business venture. With the rapid growth and evolution of 3D printing technology, the adoption of customizable and specialized products has increased significantly. This presents the ideal scenario for entrepreneurs to capitalize on the diverse market potential while also catering to the unique needs of a wide customer base.

Market Potential:

The global 3D printing market is expected to experience tremendous growth in the coming years, fueled by a robust demand for personalized and tailor-made products. Niche product offerings have become a lucrative opportunity, as customers are no longer satisfied with traditional mass-produced items. They seek products that cater to their individual requirements and preferences. Consequently, the 3D printing niche products startup can tap into a vast market segment, riding the wave of this technological revolution.

Lower Barriers of Entry:

The declining costs of 3D printers and the wide range of affordable materials, such as polymers and metals, make it easier for startups to enter the market. Small businesses can now invest in cost-effective equipment without breaking the bank, thereby lowering the barriers of entry into the industry. This increased accessibility to technology enables entrepreneurs to compete successfully in the market while producing competitive products at reasonable prices.

Environmentally Friendly:

3D printing is an eco-friendly manufacturing process, which reduces waste generated during production. This aligns with the growing demand for sustainable and environmentally friendly products. A niche 3D printing startup can capitalize on this trend by offering innovative and eco-conscious solutions to customers, further boosting the company's potential for success.

Basic Steps for Startup Success:

1. **Market Research & Niche Selection**: Conduct thorough market research to understand the needs and preferences of consumers. Choose a niche that has high demand while providing the potential for differentiation and customization.

2. **Budgeting & Funding**: Develop a realistic budget to cover startup costs, including equipment, materials, location setup, and marketing. Seek external funding, if necessary, through avenues such as angel investors, venture capitalists or crowdfunding campaigns.

3. **The Business Plan**: Develop a comprehensive business plan that covers every aspect of the startup, including the target customer base, value proposition, marketing strategies, revenue generation, and growth plans.

4. **Procurement & Supply Chain Management**: Procure 3D printers and relevant materials, set up a supply chain system that ensures cost-effectiveness and quality assurance while reducing lead times.

5. **Manufacturing & Quality Control**: Establish a production facility and implement robust quality control processes to ensure product safety and customer satisfaction.

6. **Marketing & Sales Strategy**: Develop an attractive brand and create effective marketing strategies, including social media campaigns, trade shows, and SEO tactics. Optimize sales channels by collaborating with e-commerce platforms or establishing an online store.

7. **Operations, Management & Scaling**: Establish efficient operational processes, monitor key performance indicators, and continuously iterate to improve efficiency. As the business achieves success, explore expansion opportunities, new products, or additional markets to maintain sustainable growth.

E-commerce Automation Tools

As the e-commerce market continues to grow exponentially, leveraging automation tools for increased efficiency and profitability is vital. Starting an e-commerce automation tools start-up has tremendous potential as the industry deepens its reliance on AI-driven solutions. By executing a well-crafted plan and taking critical steps, entrepreneurs can tap into a highly successful and profitable market.

Key Reasons for E-commerce Automation Success in 2024:

1. **Increasing E-Commerce Adoption**: E-commerce platforms continue to become increasingly popular, driving the need for optimization within online retail operations. As businesses vie for market positioning, tailored automation tools become vital for scalability.

2. **Demand for Cutting-Edge Technology**: The growing need to stay competitive fosters a demand for innovative automation tools. AI/ML algorithms, robotic process automation (RPA), and advanced logistics management can streamline e-commerce businesses' workflows, providing a crucial competitive edge.

3. **Enhanced Customer Experience**: Automation streamlines customer interactions by ensuring fast, reliable, and personalized responses. Automated customer service helps e-commerce companies retain customers and maintain a positive reputation within the industry.

4. **Cost Savings**: Utilizing e-commerce automation tools can reduce overhead costs and increase profits. By automating routine tasks, businesses can redeploy team efforts towards strategy development and value-added tasks.

Basic Steps to Start an E-commerce Automation Tools Start-up:

1. **Market Research**: Conduct thorough research to identify market niches, competitors, target customers, and specific pain points within the e-commerce industry. This step will drive the creation and positioning of unique value propositions for the start-up.

2. **Product Development**: Develop a suite of scalable automation tools tailored to the research findings. Products should be user-friendly, efficient, and adaptive. Collaborate with e-commerce businesses and gather feedback during the development process to ensure a minimum viable product (MVP) that meets industry demands.

3. **Legal and Financial Groundwork**: Register the start-up, acquire appropriate licenses or permits, open business bank accounts, and arrange an accounting system to manage financial records. Additionally, consider potential funding options (e.g., angel investors or venture capital) to acquire enough working capital for business operations.

4. **Build a Strong Team**: Hire a team of skilled developers, marketing experts, and industry professionals to bring the automation products to life. The company's success will significantly depend on the team's technical expertise and industry insights.

5. **Marketing and Sales**: Promote the start-up's value proposition using multi-channel marketing strategies such as social media, content marketing, email campaigns, and search engine optimization (SEO). Collaborate with e-commerce platforms, influencers, and industry leaders to drive product adoption.

6. **Customer Support and Continuous Improvement**: Establish a reputable customer support system that provides timely technical assistance and training to users. Gather customer feedback and analytics data to refine and iterate the product, ensuring a consistent competitive edge and user satisfaction.

Subscription Box Services

The subscription box services start-up business is poised to experience significant growth and profitability in 2024 due to several factors. This model allows new businesses to capitalize on the robust online market, changing consumer preferences, technological advancements, and efficient supply chain management. To be successful, budding entrepreneurs must take certain fundamental steps to ensure their venture stands out and thrives amidst competition.

Reasons for Success and Profitability:

1. **Growing Online Market**: As e-commerce continues to surge in 2024, businesses that leverage the online market are well-positioned for success. Subscription box services cater to the needs of online shoppers, offering convenience and personalized experiences which are highly sought after.

2. **Evolving Consumer Preferences**: Consumers have consistently demonstrated their fondness for curated, tailored, and customized products delivered straight to their doorstep. Subscription box services provide highly personalized offerings that cater to various niches, and this will only become more important in 2024.

3. **Technological Advancements**: With improvements in AI and machine-learning capabilities, businesses can efficiently analyze consumer preferences and adapt their product offerings to user interests in real-time. This personalized approach results in increased retention and customer satisfaction.

4. **Efficient Supply Chain Management**: The subscription box model relies on streamlined operations and strategic partnerships with suppliers. By working closely with manufacturers and distributors, businesses can optimize supply chain management and reduce costs.

101 BEST START-UP BUSINESS IDEAS FOR 2024 ACCORDING TO ADVANCED A.I.

Basic Steps to Get Started:

1. **Idea and Market Research**: Start by defining your target niche and the types of products and services to be offered. Conduct thorough market research to identify consumer trends, market gaps, and potential competition.

2. **Business Plan**: Create a detailed business plan outlining your growth strategies, financial projections, customer acquisition methods, and supply chain management plans. This will help you anticipate potential issues and stay on track and focused during the initial stages of your business.

3. **Supplier and Product Selection**: Forge strategic partnerships with suppliers, and diligently select products to ensure your subscription box delivers value for money. It is vital to maintain a strong relationship with these suppliers to ensure steady product supply and timely delivery.

4. **Branding and Packaging**: Develop a strong brand and packaging design that reflects the unique features of your subscription box. Creative designs, thoughtful approaches, and an emphasis on sustainability will make your brand stand out and appeal to potential consumers.

5. **Digital Marketing and Customer Acquisition**: Implement a marketing strategy focused on online channels such as social media, influencer marketing, and search engine optimization. These strategies can effectively promote your subscription box service and bring in potential customers.

6. **Customer Retention and Feedback**: Focus on offering excellent customer service and encourage customer feedback. Continually improve your product offerings based on feedback to increase customer satisfaction and retention rates.

AI-Based Language Learning Software

The language learning industry has seen significant growth in recent years due to globalization, technological advancements, and increasing demand for multilingual skills. By 2024, an AI-based language learning software start-up is predicted to be highly successful and profitable, courtesy of the widespread adaptation and adoption of artificial intelligence in the education sector. Traditional language learning methods have several shortcomings that can be overcome by AI-powered tools, offering personalized learning experiences, efficient progress tracking, and enhanced learner engagement. The five basic steps to initiate this start-up are ideation, planning and research, funding, development, and marketing.

Emerging Markets and Global Demand:

As global interactions become more prevalent, there is a rising need for individuals to communicate in multiple languages, whether for business, travel, or personal reasons. This demand has fueled the growth of the language learning market, making it a potential gold mine for a start-up focusing on AI-based language learning software. It is projected to grow by CAGR of 10.2% from 2021 to 2028, providing a lucrative opportunity for entrepreneurs.

Benefits of AI Over Traditional Methods:

AI-powered language learning software addresses the limitations of traditional methods (classroom-based or self-learning through textbooks and videos) by providing personalized learning experiences, catering to an individual's specific needs, goals, and pace. AI can analyze learners' strengths and weaknesses, determining the most effective teaching strategies and providing targeted feedback. It also encourages learner engagement through interactive content, simulations, and gamification techniques.

Efficient progress tracking and assessment is another advantage, as the AI system can review assignments, monitor performance, and provide tailored feedback in real-time. This continuous feedback loop enhances learner's progress and retention.

Getting Started:

1. **Ideation**: Develop a unique idea that sets your AI-based language learning software apart from competitors. Consider the target audience, essential features, and focus on areas that address existing market gaps and solve specific user problems (e.g., focused on specific language pairs or industries).

2. **Planning and Research**: Conduct thorough market research to understand the target audience, competitors, and potential collaborators. Utilize this information to create a comprehensive business plan that outlines the strategy, objectives, projected growth, and revenue streams. Legal aspects, such as copyrights and patents, need to be considered to protect intellectual property.

3. **Funding**: To launch your start-up, you may need to secure funding through different sources such as angel investors, venture capital, grants, or crowdfunding. Create a compelling pitch deck highlighting your idea's potential, target markets, and projected returns to generate investor interest.

4. **Development**: Assemble a talented team comprising AI researchers, software developers, linguists, and UX/UI designers. Design and build an AI platform that integrates machine learning algorithms, natural language processing techniques, and a user-friendly interface focusing on customer satisfaction.

5. **Marketing**: Create a strong brand identity, and leverage various marketing channels, including social media, influencer partnerships, and content marketing, to promote your product actively. Collaborations with language schools or institutes can also provide a strategic market entry. Prepare a comprehensive launch strategy, and target specific customer segments for faster user adoption.

By leveraging the power of AI, an AI-based language learning software start-up could revolutionize the industry and become highly successful and profitable by 2024.

JAIME GEHLY

Robotics Kits and Tutorials for Kids

In 2024, a robotics kits and tutorial start-up business specifically targeting kids is poised to be highly successful and profitable. This can be attributed to a variety of factors, including rapid advancements in technology, growing interest in Science, Technology, Engineering, and Mathematics (STEM) education, and an increased awareness of the importance of preparing children for the careers of the future. The following is a one-page summary detailing the reasons for this optimistic outlook and the basic steps needed to establish and scale such a start-up business.

Market Potential:

The rising popularity of robotics competitions and programs in schools worldwide demonstrates an increased demand for high-quality, affordable, and user-friendly robotics kits and tutorials. A start-up focusing on this niche can tap into this growing market and cater to both enthusiastic parents and educators who want to prepare children for a technologically advanced workforce.

Enhanced STEM Education:

Governments and schools recognize the importance of preparing kids for future jobs associated with Industrial Revolution 4.0 by integrating STEM education into their curriculum. A business focused on providing robotics kits and tutorials for children would not only be profitable but would also directly support the efforts to promote STEM literacy and skills. These skills are increasingly valuable in the job market as industries like AI, biotechnology, and renewable energy continue to expand.

Future Workforce Demands:

As automation and advanced technology become increasingly prominent in various sectors, the demand for workers skilled in robotics and automation is expected to grow significantly. By starting a business that promotes and fosters these skills among children, the start-up would be investing in shaping future generations and helping to create a well-prepared workforce that offers an attractive return on investment.

To Get Started with a Robotics Kits and Tutorial Start-Up for Kids, the Following Steps Must be Considered:

1. **Conduct Market Research**: Begin by researching the current market trends, understanding customer preferences, gauging your potential competitors, identifying gaps in the market, and determining ideal target customers (educational institutions or individual families).

2. **Develop the Product**: Design high-quality, user-friendly, and age-appropriate robotics kits and tutorials that cater to children's developmental needs. Hire subject matter experts and educators to help ensure the efficacy and attractiveness of your products. Prioritize safety and durability when designing the kits.

3. **Establish a Business Plan**: A comprehensive business plan is essential for managing your start-up and attracting investors. Clearly outline your vision, mission, objectives, market analysis, financial projections, marketing strategy, and anticipated challenges.

4. **Secure Funding**: Look for potential funding sources, such as angel investors, venture capital firms, government grants, and crowdfunding platforms, to support your start-up's initial costs, including product development, manufacturing, and marketing.

5. **Build a Strong Team**: Hire skilled and dedicated employees, including engineers, designers, marketers, educators, and customer support staff.

6. **Marketing and Distribution Strategy**: Develop a unique branding strategy to stand out in the competitive market. Use various marketing channels, such as social media, influencers, school workshops, exhibitions, and partnerships with educational institutions, to reach your target audience. Establish efficient distribution networks to ensure product availability and timely delivery.

By leveraging market potential, preparing children for future careers, and following the outlined steps, a robotics kits and tutorial start-up for kids has great potential for success and profitability.

IoT-Based Agricultural Monitoring Solutions

AI predicts that an IoT-based agricultural monitoring solutions start-up will be highly successful and profitable. The ever-growing demand for food, climate change, and the availability of cost-effective and innovative IoT (Internet of Things) technologies make it an ideal time for startups to venture into precision farming.

Market Opportunities in Agricultural Industry:

1. **Increasing Global Food Demand**: The global population is expected to reach 9.8 billion by 2050, significantly increasing the demand for food. Deploying IoT-based agricultural monitoring solutions helps optimize farm resources, increase agricultural yield, and reduce food wastage.

2. **Climate Change**: Unpredictable climate changes adversely affect agriculture, making it crucial to develop innovative solutions for adapting to and mitigating the negative impacts on farming practices.

3. **Government Support and Incentives**: Governments around the world are actively supporting sustainable agriculture through policies, grants, and funding opportunities, creating a favorable atmosphere for IoT-based agricultural startups.

Competitive Advantage:

1. **Data-Driven Decision-Making**: IoT solutions offer real-time monitoring and data-driven management of farms, allowing farmers to make better decisions based on accurate information.

2. **Resource Optimization**: IoT technologies help farmers optimize the use of resources such as water, fertilizers, and energy, which substantially reduces operational costs and lowers the ecological footprint of agriculture.

3. **Improved Quality and Yield**: IoT-based solutions enable precise monitoring of crop health and environmental conditions, facilitating early detection and treatment of issues such as pests and plant diseases. This results in improved crop quality and yield.

Steps to Start an IoT-based Agricultural Monitoring Solutions Startup:

1. **Market Research**: Conduct extensive research to identify customer needs, target audience, and competitors.

2. **Develop a Unique Value Proposition**: Create an innovative and differentiated offering that stands out in the market and meets customer needs.

3. **Build a Strong Team**: Assemble a skilled and motivated team comprising IoT experts, agronomists, data analysts, and software developers to work collaboratively toward the company's goals.

4. **Secure Funding**: Explore various funding options such as government grants, venture capital, angel investors, and crowdfunding to raise capital to establish and grow the business.

5. **Design and Develop the Solution**: Develop an IoT-based agricultural monitoring system that includes hardware sensors, data communication networks, data storage, and data analytics capabilities.

6. **Establish Partner Network**: Collaborate with other players in the ecosystem such as hardware manufacturers, network providers, and agricultural organizations to enhance the overall offering, improve management practices, and gain access to valuable resources.

7. **Test and Validate**: Run pilot tests and collect feedback from early users to refine the solution, ensuring it adheres to industry standards and meets customer demands.

8. **Launch and Scale the Business**: Successfully market the solution and expand the customer base. Consider scaling up through franchising, licensing, strategic partnerships, or acquisitions to grow the business further.

An IoT-based agricultural monitoring solutions startup in 2024 will capitalize on the need for sustainable and efficient agricultural practices in the face of global challenges like population growth and climate change. Through careful planning, product development, and strategic partnerships, startups can seize this opportunity and contribute to revolutionizing the agricultural industry while generating significant profits.

Smart Kitchen Appliances

A smart kitchen appliances start-up business in 2024 is poised for high success and profitability due to the fast-growing demand for technological advancements in the kitchen space, increasing focus on energy efficiency, and a strong consumer appetite for connected living. By creating innovative, user-friendly and energy-efficient smart appliances, budding entrepreneurs can carve a niche in this ever-evolving market. This summary outlines the reasons for potential success and key steps for getting started in this lucrative venture.

Market Growth and Demand:

1. **Technological Advancements**: With increasing research and development, kitchen appliances are continuously evolving, bringing forth smart solutions that save time, energy, and resources. This creates a lucrative market for innovative start-ups that can cater to consumers' changing needs.

2. **Energy Efficiency**: As global energy consumption continues to rise; the importance of energy-efficient solutions has become paramount. A start-up that focuses on producing smart kitchen appliances with lower energy consumption will garner significant attention and success.

3. **Connected Living**: With the Internet of Things (IoT) gaining traction, consumers are seeking seamless integration of their appliances with other household devices. A smart kitchen appliances start-up that can offer unified, easily manageable systems is likely to thrive.

To Get Started:

1. **Market Research**: Conduct thorough research on current trends, consumer preferences, and competitors in the smart kitchen appliances market. Determine the potential gaps to develop innovative products that fill unmet customer needs.

2. **Defining Product Range**: Based on the market research, select a range of smart kitchen appliances that demonstrate high consumer demand and growth potential. Aim to create unique and value-added products that differentiate your start-up from competitors.

3. **Legal and Financial Aspects**: Set up your legal structure, such as registering your company and acquiring necessary licenses and permits. Develop a financial plan that outlines your start-up costs, funding sources, break-even analysis, and projected revenue streams.

4. **Supply Chain Management**: Establish relationships with reliable suppliers, manufacturers, and distributors who can ensure quality products at cost-effective rates. Good supply chain management is crucial for maintaining an efficient and profitable business.

5. **R&D and Innovation**: Constantly invest in research and development to stay ahead of the competition. Create a team of experts who can develop innovative smart kitchen solutions and improve existing products.

6. **Marketing and Promotional Activities**: Develop a comprehensive marketing plan that encompasses online and offline strategies. Leverage social media, influencer marketing, and industry trade shows to showcase your products and engage with potential customers.

7. **Customer Support**: Establish excellent customer service and after-sales support systems to ensure consumer satisfaction and encourage word-of-mouth recommendations.

A smart kitchen appliances start-up in 2024 offers an enticing business opportunity, driven by consumer demand for advanced, energy-efficient, and integrated appliances. Entrepreneurs who can strategically capitalize on this market by offering innovative products and exceptional customer experiences are well-positioned for high success.

AI-Driven Virtual Event Platform

In 2024, an AI-driven virtual event platform start-up is poised to be a lucrative and trendsetting business venture. In an era defined by widespread digitalization, remote work, and connectivity, this innovative solution offers immense benefits, such as cost savings, increased engagement, and seamless personalization. The start-up's success hinges on thorough market research, effective development and integration of cutting-edge AI features, smart marketing strategies, and a commitment to customer satisfaction.

Market Growth and Opportunities:

An increasing number of companies and other major stakeholders are opting for virtual events over traditional in-person gatherings due to travel restrictions, cost reductions, and convenience. This shift is even more pronounced post-COVID-19 pandemic, as many organizations have adapted to working remotely. As a result, the demand for innovative, immersive, and engaging event solutions is greater than ever.

The AI Advantage:

By integrating AI technology, an AI-driven virtual event platform start-up can deliver a range of game-changing features. AI-powered chatbots facilitate intelligent and instantaneous communication, providing the best possible customer support. Advanced personalization features eliminate potential logistical hitches, while real-time language translation removes barriers to entry, thereby enabling a more diverse and global audience to participate in events. Meanwhile, AI-driven analytics help organizers make better, data-based strategic decisions and tailor content to meet attendees' preferences and needs.

Steps to Get Started:

1. **Market Research and Analysis**: First and foremost, a thorough understanding of the market, including its size, trends, and consumer preferences, is crucial. Identify major players, analyze their strengths and weaknesses, and search for gaps in the market or areas of potential growth.

2. **Unique Value Proposition**: Develop a clear unique value proposition that sets the platform apart from competitors. By leveraging AI, scalability, and security features, create a platform that appeals to various event types, including conferences, trade shows, educational events, and job fairs.

3. **Comprehensive Business Plan**: Prepare a detailed business plan that outlines the budget, revenue projections, team structure, intellectual property protections, and promotional strategies. This document will serve as a roadmap for the start-up, helping to attract investors and strategic partners.

4. **Build an Expert Team**: Assemble a skilled team that melds expertise in software development, AI technology, and project management. This will ensure effective product development, marketing efforts, and execution of the overall business plan.

5. **Implement AI Features**: Transparency and accuracy are important when integrating AI features. Work closely with software engineers to create and sow components, while testing for performance, usability, and adaptability.

6. **Marketing and Promotion**: Generate hype around the product with a well-crafted marketing plan that emphasizes the AI-driven nature of the platform. Focus on SEO, content marketing, social media campaigns, and strategic partnerships with relevant influencers or organizations to create a buzz and generate leads.

7. **Iterate and Improve**: Following the platform's launch, commit to continuous improvement, staying up-to-date on emerging technologies and responding to user feedback. Incorporate client suggestions and enhance functionalities to ensure long-term success.

In conclusion, an AI-driven virtual event platform start-up is an exceptional business opportunity given the rise of remote experiences and digital connectivity. By executing these steps effectively, entrepreneurs can tap into this profitable niche market and drive lasting success.

Chatbot-Based E-Commerce

Chatbot-based e-commerce start-ups are poised to be highly lucrative business ventures, capitalizing on the advancements in artificial intelligence (AI) technology, changing consumer trends, and the increasing digital ecosystem. These chatbots directly communicate and engage with customers, improving online shopping experiences and leading to higher revenue growth for e-commerce businesses.

Market Landscape:

1. **Growing E-Commerce Market**: The e-commerce sector is expected to show consistent growth through 2024, providing a fertile ground for innovative solutions, including chatbot-based platforms.

2. **Increasing Smartphone Penetration**: The widespread use of smartphones globally leads to more digital interactions and higher demand for e-commerce services, thus increasing the potential revenue for chatbot-driven companies.

3. **Millennial and Gen Z Consumers**: These younger generations, who are digitally native, prefer quick, personalized, and seamless shopping experiences that chatbots can easily deliver.

Key Benefits of Chatbot-Driven E-commerce Platforms:

1. **Enhanced Customer Experience**: By providing instant responses, personalized recommendations, and resolving queries in real time, chatbots significantly improve customer satisfaction levels.

2. **Cost Efficiency**: Chatbots are operational 24/7, reducing the need for large customer service teams and lowering overall operational costs.

3. **Higher Sales Conversion**: Chatbots can effectively generate leads and guide customers through the sales funnel, driving higher conversion rates and increased revenue.

Basic Steps to Launch a Chatbot-Based E-commerce Start-up:

1. **Market Research and Niche Identification**: Identify trends and determine a specific target market and product niche to focus on. Understand the needs and preferences of your audience to develop tailored chatbot solutions.

2. **Selection of Chatbot Platform/Framework**: Choose the appropriate platform or framework to build your chatbot. Consider factors such as cost, ease of use, and scalability.

3. **Building a Technologically Competent Team**: Bring together a skilled and diverse team, including AI developers, data analysts, marketers, and customer service experts, to support your chatbot-driven business.

4. **Create and Train the Chatbot**: Design an engaging conversational interface, ensuring the bot has a friendly personality, and train the chatbot using AI algorithms to improve its language and problem-solving capabilities.

5. **Integration with E-commerce Platform and CRM**: Seamlessly integrate the chatbot into your existing e-commerce platform and customer relationship management (CRM) system, so it can smoothly access relevant data and automate various tasks.

6. **Testing and Improvements**: Rigorously test the chatbot to identify and rectify its limitations, and continuously iterate to maintain its usability and effectiveness.

7. **Marketing and Promotion**: Develop a comprehensive multi-channel marketing plan to create awareness of your chatbot-based e-commerce start-up and differentiate it from competitors.

Given the predicted market growth, changing consumer preferences, and the potential advantages offered by chatbots in e-commerce, launching a chatbot-based start-up has great potential for strong revenue growth. By identifying the right niche, assembling the right team, and constantly improving your chatbot, your e-commerce business will be well-positioned for success in the digital landscape.

Voice Command Applications

Starting a voice command applications start-up business is a smart and successful choice due to the rapid growth and development of the voice technology market. With voice assistants quickly gaining traction and an increasing number of devices integrating voice control, now is the right time to capitalize on this trend. In order to ensure a successful start, one must follow a series of steps that include validating the idea, creating a strong business plan, assembling a skilled team, developing the technology, and advertising the product.

Growing Market for Voice Technology:

The global voice technology market has experienced remarkable growth in the past few years, proving the popularity of voice assistants like Amazon's Alexa, Google Assistant, and Apple's Siri. These assistants have increasingly been integrated into smart devices, highlighting the incorporation of voice control mechanisms in various sectors. The trend for a more seamless, intuitive, and convenient human-device interaction is expected to continue, opening opportunities for voice command application start-ups to dominate the market.

Validate the Voice Command Application Idea:

Before launching a start-up, it is crucial to validate the idea by conducting market research and identifying the target customer segment. This research should help identify market gaps and areas where voice command applications can provide the most value. Ensure the idea aligns with the current market trends and customer preferences for a higher likelihood of success.

Steps to Launch a Voice Command Applications Start-up:

Create a Comprehensive Business Plan: A well-structured business plan is essential for providing direction and securing funding. The plan should outline the company's mission, goals, target market, competition analysis, marketing strategy, financial projections, and a timeline for development and launch. This document is critical when seeking funding from investors and when measuring the business's progress and success.

Assemble a Skilled and Diverse Team: A strong and capable team is one of the key components to successfully launching a voice command applications start-up. Recruit skilled professionals with expertise in artificial intelligence, machine learning, natural language processing, software development, UX/UI design, and project management. A diverse team will bring complementary skills and offer creative problem-solving approaches.

Develop the Voice Command Application: Once the foundations are in place, invest in developing the technology. The development process includes designing, coding, and testing the voice command application, with a focus on excellent user experience and compatibility with popular devices and operating systems. Ensure the application provides value and solves problems faced by the target market.

Marketing and Advertising: To promote the application and gain traction, develop a comprehensive marketing strategy. Utilize social media, content marketing, influencer collaborations, and public relations to generate awareness and excitement around the product. Targeted advertising, app store optimization, and possible partnerships with device manufacturers can lead to increased visibility and higher adoption rates.

In conclusion, launching a voice command applications start-up is a smart choice due to the forecasted growth of the voice technology market. By validating the idea, creating a robust business plan, assembling a skilled team, developing the technology, and effectively marketing the final product, entrepreneurs can position themselves for success in this fast-growing digital landscape.

VR/AR-Based Escape Rooms

Virtual reality (VR) and augmented reality (AR) technologies have seen significant advancements in recent years, creating countless opportunities for businesses across various industries. One such opportunity is establishing a VR/AR-based escape room start-up business. By combining the excitement of escape rooms with the captivating nature of VR and AR, entrepreneurs can offer a unique and immersive experience for customers, ensuring a smart and successful business.

Reasons for Success:

1. **Rising Popularity of VR/AR**: The global VR/AR market is projected to reach significant growth in the coming years, as both consumer and enterprise applications become more popular. With rapidly improving hardware capabilities and more accessible price points, VR/AR-based escape rooms will present a niche yet lucrative business opportunity.

2. **Unique Experience for Customers**: The immersive nature of VR/AR technology can create experiences beyond those offered in traditional escape rooms. Customers can be transported to various environments and landscapes, allowing for much more creative and exciting scenarios.

3. **Enhanced Safety Precautions**: Given the concerns about health and safety, VR/AR-based escape rooms can offer safe environments for people to enjoy. Such establishments may require minimal physical interaction, reducing the risk of spreading germs and making the concept more appealing to health-conscious customers.

4. **Expandable Business Model**: As VR/AR technologies advance, additional content and experiences can be created and offered to customers, ensuring a constantly evolving and engaging experience. This flexibility provides a strong foundation for potential business expansion.

Basic Steps to Get Started:

1. **Extensive Market Research**: Understanding the target audience and competition helps to identify opportunities and threats in the market. It is essential to analyze escape room trends, customer preferences, and potential business locations.

2. **Establishing a Business Plan**: A solid business plan that incorporates marketing, financial forecasting, funding requirements, and operations is crucial for the long-term success of the venture. This plan should outline the company's goals, milestones, and strategies for success.

3. **Identifying Technology Partnerships**: Given the reliance on VR/AR technologies, finding suitable hardware and software partners is vital. Collaborating with companies that have expertise in developing immersive VR/AR experiences can ensure high-quality content for the escape rooms.

4. **Securing Funding**: The capital required for the initial setup and operation of a VR/AR-based escape room business may be significant. Assessing various funding options, such as loans, crowdfunding, or angel investment, is crucial to meeting budgetary goals.

5. **Acquiring Licenses and Permits**: Ensure all necessary business permits, licenses, and insurance coverages are obtained before launching the venture to prevent potential legal issues.

6. **Creating Engaging Experiences**: Collaborate with designers, storytellers, and software developers to create immersive VR/AR-based escape room scenarios that are both challenging and entertaining for customers.

7. **Marketing and Promotion**: Developing a comprehensive marketing strategy using both online and offline channels can generate awareness, drive customer engagement, and establish brand identity. Social media marketing, search engine optimization, and partnerships with influencers are key components of effective marketing efforts.

In conclusion, the VR/AR-based escape room start-up is a smart and viable business idea, offering unique experiences within a growing market. Executing a well-researched strategy, efficient operations, and providing exceptional customer experiences are key to long-term success in this emerging industry.

JAIME GEHLY

Blockchain-Based Supply Chain Management

In today's globalized economy, supply-chain management (SCM) is vital to drive business success. As the industry continues to evolve, the adoption of innovative technologies such as blockchain has become crucial for maintaining a competitive edge. A blockchain-based supply chain management start-up would harness the technology's potential to address current SCM challenges and create new business opportunities. The essential steps required to get started include identifying the niche, building a team, creating a minimum viable product (MVP), conducting market research, and securing funding.

The rapid growth of international trade and globalization has made supply-chain management increasingly complex. Companies face multiple challenges regarding efficiency, transparency, and security. Blockchain technology has emerged as a viable solution to these concerns, making the establishment of a blockchain-based supply chain management start-up a viable and promising business idea.

Blockchain and Supply Chain Management:

Blockchain, the distributed ledger technology, allows organizations to trace the movement of goods within the supply chain from production to final delivery. It ensures end-to-end visibility, data accuracy, and security by providing a transparent, decentralized platform for recording transactions and sharing real-time information. Blockchain can transform the operations of the traditional supply chain by:

1. **Enhancing Traceability**: Blockchain allows suppliers, manufacturers, and retailers to track assets and products throughout the entire supply chain. This enhanced traceability can improve efficiency, ensure the authenticity of the products, and address issues related to counterfeiting and fraud.

2. **Increasing Transparency**: The distributed nature of blockchain ensures transparency in sharing information with all parties involved in the supply chain. Every transaction is visible, which minimizes fraud and builds trust among stakeholders.

3. **Streamlining Processes**: Blockchain simplifies the management of complex supply chain networks by automating documentation and administrative tasks, thereby reducing costs and minimizing human errors.

4. **Strengthening Security**: Blockchain provides a secure platform for data management by using a cryptographic hash that protects against tampering and unauthorized access.

Getting Started:

1. **Identify the Niche**: Determine the specific supply chain domain that the business will cater to, such as pharmaceuticals, consumer goods, or automotive industries.

2. **Build a Team**: Assemble a team of experts with diverse skill sets, including blockchain development, supply chain management, and business development.

3. **Develop a Minimum Viable Product (MVP)**: Design and develop an initial version of the product or platform that demonstrates the use of blockchain in solving SCM-related issues.

4. **Conduct Market Research**: Study the market to gather insights about customer needs, potential competitors, and collaborative opportunities with existing organizations in the supply chain domain.

5. **Secure Funding**: Explore various funding sources, such as angel investors, venture capital firms, and crowdfunding platforms, or consider partnering with established companies to develop the product and scale the business.

A blockchain-based supply-chain management start-up can leverage the innovative capabilities of the technology to deliver end-to-end visibility, transparency, and security in the supply chain.

VR-based Travel Experiences

In recent years, numerous technological advancements have been made, including the incredible growth in virtual reality (VR) applications. With the impact of the COVID-19 pandemic on the travel industry, the world has become aware of the importance of immersive experiences in a safe, controlled environment. This report outlines why launching a VR-based travel experiences start-up would be a smart and successful choice, as well as covers the essential steps to get started.

Reasons for Success:

1. **Market Demand**: Due to limitations on international travel during and after the pandemic, there has been a surge in demand for alternative experiences. A VR-based start-up can provide customers with the ability to explore various global destinations without leaving their homes, thereby satisfying their wanderlust and tapping into this booming market.

2. **Cost-Effective for Customers**: In comparison to traditional travel, a VR-based experience can provide an affordable alternative, appealing to a wide range of customers. It would allow cost-conscious individuals to explore various global destinations easily, experiencing them to their fullest extent without any financial constraints.

3. **Sustainable Travel**: As climate change and environmental issues come to the forefront, VR-based start-ups can offer more sustainable, eco-friendly travel options, allowing people to appreciate and learn about different parts of the world while reducing their carbon footprint.

4. **Technological Evolution**: With the rapid development of VR technology, immersive experiences have become increasingly realistic and engaging. This new technology would give the start-up the competitive edge in creating memorable experiences for clients.

Basic Steps to Get Started:

1. **Market Research**: Initially, thorough market research is vital to understand the target audience, competition, and potential challenges for your VR-based start-up. This will help in planning out effective strategies to cater to your target demographic.

2. **Develop a Unique Selling Proposition (USP)**: Identify what sets your start-up apart from existing competition in the marketplace. Focus on what unique value or innovative experiences you can offer customers in comparison to traditional travel options or other VR-based businesses.

3. **Establish Partnerships**: Form partnerships with VR technology developers, travel agencies, and tourist organizations. These relationships will allow for collaboration and help create immersive content, develop innovative experiences, and market the start-up more effectively.

4. **Legalities and Compliance**: Acquire the necessary permits, licenses, and registrations for your start-up. These will ensure that your business operates in compliance with the relevant laws and regulations, while also avoiding any potential legal issues in the future.

5. **Develop a Comprehensive Marketing Strategy**: To successfully launch your start-up, design and implement a marketing plan that takes advantage of both traditional and digital marketing methods, targeting your identified audience segments. Use social media, PR, and promotional events to generate buzz and increase awareness about your unique offerings.

6. **Develop and Test the Product**: Once your business model is in place, work with the technical team and subject matter experts to design, develop, and test the VR experiences. It is essential to keep refining and iterating on user feedback, ensuring the best possible experience for customers.

In conclusion, 2024 capitalizes on the global shift in travel habits, addresses environmental concerns, and meets the insatiable demand for unique, immersive experiences.

IoT-Based Home Automation Systems

An IoT-based home automation system start-up has immense potential for success. With the increasing global adoption of smart home devices and the expanding possibilities of the Internet of Things (IoT) ecosystem, demand for innovative and user-friendly home automation solutions will continue to surge. This document details the reasons behind this success and outlines the basic steps for starting such a business.

Reasons for Success:

1. **Rising Consumer Demand**: The growing preference for smart, connected homes is fueling the demand for IoT-based home automation systems. Proliferating technology awareness and increasing disposable income contribute to the attraction of intelligent devices that offer convenience, comfort, and security.

2. **Expansion of The IoT Ecosystem**: The IoT technology landscape will continue to evolve and broaden, enabling home automation systems to incorporate an even wider array of devices and applications. As a result, system integration and seamless interoperability will become crucial for creating unified solutions, providing ample opportunities for innovation.

3. **Energy Efficiency**: Eco-conscious consumers seek energy-efficient options to reduce their environmental impact and save on utility bills. IoT-based home automation systems can offer this through smart energy management, lighting control, and temperature monitoring.

4. **Enhanced Security and Privacy**: Homeowners are increasingly concerned about property security and privacy protection. IoT-based home automation solutions can offer advanced security features, such as AI-enabled cameras, smart locks, and access control systems, to address these issues.

5. **Favorable Regulatory Environment**: Governments worldwide are increasingly promoting the adoption of smart home technologies to conserve resources and address environmental concerns. Favorable policies and incentives will encourage the growth of the home automation industry in 2024.

Basic Steps to Get Started:

1. **Market Research**: Survey the current market landscape and gather insights into existing competitors, potential customers, and common pain points or limitations needing improvement.

2. **Business Plan**: Create a comprehensive business plan detailing your start-up's organizational structure, marketing, and operational strategies, growth projections, funding requirements, and financial projections.

3. **Product Development**: Assemble a skilled team to design and develop innovative, secure, and user-friendly IoT-based home automation systems that answer specific consumer needs.

4. **Collaboration with Industry Partners**: Partner with renowned IoT device manufacturers, home security companies, and software developers to identify complementary products and solutions for integration. This collaboration will ensure compatibility and improve the value proposition.

5. **Regulatory Compliance**: Acquire relevant licenses or certifications, and ensure compliance with governmental regulations, privacy laws, and industry standards.

6. **Marketing and Sales**: Develop a result-driven marketing strategy, utilizing digital channels, trade shows, and targeted advertising to attract potential customers. Establish a robust sales network, including online platforms, distributors, and collaborations with builders and real estate developers.

7. **Customer Support and Service**: Provide exceptional customer support and after-sales service to enhance customer satisfaction, promoting retention and word-of-mouth advertising.

In summary, the rising consumer demand for smart homes, continuous IoT ecosystem expansion, focus on energy efficiency, increased security requirements, and supportive governmental policies place the IoT-based home automation business within an opportune success trajectory in 2024 and beyond. Following the above steps and staying committed to innovation will pave the way for a thriving and impactful start-up in the home automation industry.

QR-Code Based Contactless Payments

The prevalence of contactless payments is increasing at an exponential rate, and the trend is expected to persist in 2024. A start-up focusing on QR-code based contactless payment solutions will be successful and profitable, given the gradually evolving payments landscape and emerging customer demands. This paper summarizes the key factors driving the success of this start-up, along with the basic steps required to initiate the business.

Key Factors Driving Success:

1. **Market Trends and Demand**: The global pandemic has accelerated the adoption of digital and contactless payment methods, and people are more comfortable with their use in day-to-day transactions. Retailers are looking for efficient, contactless solutions to keep up with this demand, ensuring ample market opportunities for this start-up.

2. **Cost-Effective Implementation**: QR codes are a low-cost alternative to Near Field Communication (NFC) and other contactless payment methods. Merchants and users can easily generate QR codes without the need for investing in costly infrastructure. This affordability appeals to a broad customer base and ensures profitability.

3. **Cross-Platform Compatibility**: QR-code based contactless payments are compatible across various devices, including smartphones, tablets, and point-of-sale (POS) systems. This broad compatibility fosters rapid adoption by consumers and businesses, thus ensuring the success of the start-up.

4. **Security and Fraud Prevention**: Modern QR-code based contactless payment solutions employ end-to-end encryption and tokenization to secure transactions. They can also implement features such as biometric authentication for additional security measures. Consumers and businesses are likely to opt for a secure and convenient solution, thereby leading to profitability.

Basic Steps to Get Started:

1. **Conduct Market Research**: Before starting, perform comprehensive market research to understand the existing competition, target customer base, and potential collaborations. This information will help establish a strong business plan and identify valuable market opportunities.

2. **Develop the QR-Code Based Payment Platform**: Collaborate with experienced developers and engineers to create a user-friendly, fast, and secure contactless payment platform. Integrating features like loyalty programs and multi-currency support can also enhance its appeal.

3. **Establish Strategic Partnerships**: Partner with financial institutions, card networks, and merchant aggregators to provide seamless and integrated financial services. Creating a network of supportive business partners will contribute to long-term success and scalability.

4. **Obtain Regulatory Approvals and Legal Requirements**: Comply with local and international financial regulations and obtain necessary licenses and certifications to operate in the desired locations. Staying compliant ensures that the platform maintains a reputable status in the market.

5. **Launch and Marketing**: Develop a strategic marketing plan to create brand awareness and promote the start-up's QR-code based contactless payment solutions. Utilize online advertising, social media, influencer collaborations, and publicity events to reach your target audience effectively.

The market for QR-code based contactless payment solutions is poised to flourish in 2024 and beyond, presenting a unique opportunity for start-ups to enter the industry. By addressing market trends, providing cost-effective solutions, ensuring compatibility and security, and following the outlined steps, a QR-code based contactless payments start-up can successfully establish itself as a profitable business venture.

JAIME GEHLY

Cybersecurity Services for Small Businesses

Establishing a cybersecurity services start-up for small businesses is particularly lucrative and poised for success due to the rapid increase in cyber threats, growing internet dependency, and accelerating adoption of digital technologies. Small businesses often lack the expertise, resources, and infrastructure to effectively defend against the ever-evolving cyber threat landscape, leaving them particularly vulnerable to attacks. By addressing this burgeoning demand, a cybersecurity services start-up can tap into a lucrative and underserved market niche, making it both successful and profitable.

Key Factors:

1. **Cyber Threats on the Rise**: Incidents of data breaches, ransomware attacks, and other cyber exploitations are escalating at an alarming rate. Small businesses are attractive targets for cybercriminals because they often possess valuable data but lack robust security measures. As a result, there is strong demand for effective cybersecurity solutions to protect small businesses and mitigate potential financial and reputational losses.

2. **Digital Transformation and IoT Adoption**: The rapid digital transformation experienced by businesses around the globe has been fueled by the adoption of cloud services, mobile technologies, and the Internet of Things (IoT). Small businesses are more reliant on digital technologies than ever before, driving the need for comprehensive cybersecurity services to secure their IT infrastructure and connected devices from cyber threats.

3. **Cost-Effective and Scalable Solutions**: Small businesses have limited budgets and require cost-effective and scalable cybersecurity solutions. A start-up that can provide tailored services to address the unique needs of each client, leveraging emerging technologies such as machine learning and artificial intelligence for threat detection, will be well-positioned for success.

4. **Government Regulations and Compliance**: Stringent government regulations force small businesses to invest in and adhere to cybersecurity standards and guidelines. This creates a constant demand for security audits, consulting, and technical support, generating numerous business opportunities in the compliance landscape.

To Successfully Set Up a Cybersecurity Services Start-Up for Small Businesses in 2024, The Following Basic Steps Are Essential:

1. **Business Planning and Research**: Develop a well-structured business plan that outlines target markets, competition analysis, service offerings, business model, and sales strategy. Perform extensive market research to identify the specific needs of small businesses and potential growth sectors.

2. **Establishing Expertise**: Build or hire a team with specialized knowledge in cybersecurity, including professionals in risk assessment, threat analysis, vulnerability testing, secure development practices, incident response, and user training.

3. **Legal Compliance and Registration**: Ensure legal compliance by registering the start-up, obtaining necessary licenses and permits, and keeping up-to-date with local, state, and federal regulations.

4. **Building a Strong Brand**: Create a consistent brand identity and marketing strategy to effectively communicate the value and expertise of your cybersecurity services start-up. This will help establish trust and credibility among potential clients.

5. **Networking and Partnerships**: Attend industry conferences, workshops, and social events to expand your network and forge strategic partnerships. Partner with like-minded service providers to offer complementary solutions to clients.

In conclusion, a cybersecurity services start-up for small businesses in 2024 has enormous potential for success and profitability. By staying abreast of emerging trends, harnessing cutting-edge technologies, and tapping into growing market demand, a cybersecurity start-up can be well-positioned to secure long-term business growth and client success.

JAIME GEHLY

AI-Driven Biotech Research

The exponential growth of biotechnology, coupled with the rapid advancement in artificial intelligence (AI), presents a unique and promising opportunity for an AI-driven biotech research start-up in 2024. Combining these technologies positions the start-up for success by accelerating drug discovery, providing personalized medicine, enhancing research efficiency, and increasing profitability. The basic steps to get started include identifying niche focus, securing funding, assembling a team, and implementing AI-driven research technologies.

The global biotechnology market is expected to grow steadily, reaching an estimated $1.7 trillion by 2028. The demand for personalized medicine, advanced drug discovery, and cost-effective research and development will continue to increase, making a significant market opportunity for AI-driven biotech research start-ups.

Key Factors:

1. **Accelerated Drug Discovery**: AI-driven biotech start-ups have the potential to revolutionize the drug discovery process, reducing time and costs by predicting the outcomes of complex chemical interactions, identifying potential drug candidates, and optimizing drug synthesis. This acceleration will lead to quicker validation of effective drug compounds, resulting in faster time-to-market and heightened profitability.

2. **Personalized Medicine**: By 2024, personalized medicine will be more prevalent, as patients demand tailor-made treatment plans based on their genetics and lifestyle factors. AI-driven biotech start-ups will be well-positioned to support this growing demand through data analysis and computational modeling, enabling healthcare providers to offer individualized medical solutions.

3. **Enhanced Research Efficiency**: AI can optimize research in biotechnology by minimizing human biases and streamlining data analysis, allowing for better interpretation of results and more accurate predictions. This increased efficiency leads to a reduction in research and development costs, enhancing the start-up's profitability.

4. **Growing Profitability**: AI-driven biotech research start-ups will capitalize on the increasing market demand for advanced drugs, therapies, and gene editing

technologies, resulting in increasing profitability. AI-powered research will reduce costs and the risk of failure while creating new business opportunities in medical diagnostics and treatments.

Basic Steps to Get Started:

1. **Identify Niche Focus**: To thrive in a competitive market, identify a niche focus within biotechnology that is underserved or has the potential to be transformed by AI-driven research, such as drug discovery, gene editing, or biomaterials synthesis.

2. **Secure Funding**: Seek out investors or grants to secure sufficient funding for the start-up, emphasizing the market opportunities and competitive advantage resulting from the AI-driven biotech research approach.

3. **Assemble a Team**: Build a multidisciplinary team comprising experts in biotechnology, computer science, data analytics, and AI, along with an experienced management team to handle business development and operations.

4. **Implement AI-Driven Research Technologies**: Integrate cutting-edge AI platforms and algorithms, such as machine learning, natural language processing, and deep learning, to support and enhance biotechnology research.

In conclusion, an AI-driven biotech research start-up will be ideally positioned to successfully compete in the rapidly growing biotechnology sector in 2024. By leveraging AI technology, these start-ups will disrupt the industry, delivering advanced pharmaceuticals, therapies, and medical insights that will ultimately lead to increased profitability and impact in a rapidly evolving market.

Live Streaming Platforms and Tools

In recent years, live streaming has become an integral part of the digital landscape as more creators and businesses rely on real-time content to build communities, engage with customers, and promote their services. This rapid growth and adoption have created a demand for innovative live streaming platforms and tools that cater to diverse needs. A start-up focusing on live streaming platforms and tools has a high probability of success and profitability in 2024, thanks to increased internet penetration, the influence of social media, and the evolving landscape of consumer culture. To capitalize on this opportunity, a start-up can follow a series of basic steps to successfully create and market its services.

Factors Driving the Success and Profitability of a Live Streaming Start-Up in 2024:

1. **Widespread Internet Access**: A driving force behind the success of live streaming platforms is global internet penetration. By 2024, more people will have access to high-speed internet, enabling them to consume live content easily and fuel demand for such services.

2. **Social Media Influence**: Social media platforms, e-commerce sites, and online communities are increasingly facilitating the integration of live streaming content. This development continues to create opportunities for start-ups to develop new platforms and tools dedicated to live streaming.

3. **eSports and Gaming**: The eSports and gaming industries are growing exponentially, resulting in a massive demand for live streaming platforms that cater to gamers and fans. This target market offers ample opportunity for innovative businesses to thrive in 2024.

4. **Diverse Applications and Use Cases**: Live streaming has diverse applications across various sectors, such as education, entertainment, marketing, and fitness. A start-up that offers innovative platforms and tools can tap into these markets to increase profitability.

Basic Steps to Get Started:

1. **Identifying the Target Market**: First, determine the target market for your live streaming platform/tool – eSports and gaming, fitness, e-commerce, or education. Thorough market research will help in selecting the most profitable niche and crafting a tailored platform experience.

2. **Developing the Platform and Tools**: Once the target market is identified, collaborate with a technical team to develop the live streaming platform and tools. Ensure that the platform is user-friendly, responsive, and offers features that cater to the specific needs of your audience.

3. **Protecting Intellectual Property**: Secure patents, trademarks, and copyrights for your platform and tools to maintain control over your brand and prevent copycat products from entering the market.

4. **Creating a Marketing Strategy**: Develop a comprehensive marketing strategy to promote your start-up, raise awareness of your services, and acquire users for your platform. Leverage content marketing, social media advertising, influencer partnerships, and targeted advertising to reach your ideal audience.

5. **Establishing Partnerships**: Collaborate with third-party content creators, publishers, and influencers in your niche – this helps drive user traffic and generate organic growth for your live streaming platform.

6. **Monetization**: Decide on the revenue streams for your platform, such as paid subscriptions, advertising, or a combination of both. Experiment with different monetization models to find the most profitable fit for your start-up.

In conclusion, the burgeoning live streaming industry offers a lucrative opportunity for a start-up in 2024. Identifying the right niche, developing an innovative platform or tool, and effectively marketing it are crucial keys to success and profitability in this rapidly expanding market.

AI-Based Emotion Recognition Technology

The development of Artificial Intelligence (AI) and machine learning technologies has greatly impacted various industries and continues to bring groundbreaking innovations. One of these domains is emotion recognition, where AI recognizes and interprets human emotions from text, speech, facial expressions, and other physiological indicators. In 2024, an AI-based emotion recognition startup has numerous potential applications, making it a promising business opportunity.

Market Opportunity:

The demand for AI-based emotion recognition technology is growing rapidly due to its wide applicability in various sectors, including human resources, advertising, customer service, health and wellness, education, and entertainment. In the age of remote work and customer-centric approaches, understanding and analyzing human emotions is invaluable for providing personalized services, enhancing user experience, and improving overall communication. This technology could also help monitor mental health, facilitate employee wellbeing, and track user engagement in e-learning, further driving market growth.

Basic Steps to Start an AI-Based Emotion Recognition Startup:

1. **Research and Identify the Market Niche**: Analyze the existing competitive landscape and identify the areas or industries where AI-based emotion recognition technology could provide the most significant value, and focus on creating a unique offering or advancing upon the existing solutions.

2. **Develop the Business Plan**: Define the company's mission, vision, target market, revenue model, and create a detailed roadmap for product development, marketing, and customer acquisition. While formulating the plan, make sure to consider potential roadblocks, such as data privacy, ethical concerns, and regulatory frameworks.

3. **Assemble the Founding Team**: Hire skilled specialists, including machine learning engineers, data scientists, domain experts, and business development professionals. Establish a multidisciplinary team that combines technical, business, and ethical acumen, ensuring a well-rounded foundation for the startup.

4. **Secure Funding**: Explore and secure sources of funding to support the company's research, development, and operations. This may include angel investors, venture capital firms, government grants, or crowdfunding platforms. Present a compelling pitch that addresses the market demand, your solution's benefits, and the potential return on investment.

5. **Develop the Emotion Recognition Technology**: Leverage machine learning techniques, such as deep learning and natural language processing (NLP), to develop emotion recognition models that can be trained on large datasets. Collaborate with experts from the target industries to ensure that the technology meets their specific needs and requirements.

6. **Obtain Necessary Approvals and Certifications**: Comply with relevant international, federal, and regional laws and regulations concerning data privacy, AI ethics, and cybersecurity. Obtain any required certifications, particularly for industries where regulatory compliance is critical, like healthcare, finance, or education.

7. **Launch a Minimum Viable Product (MVP)**: Before investing significant resources into the final product, create and launch an MVP to gather early customer feedback and refine your offering based on their input. This approach helps minimize risks, optimize resources, and ensures that the product aligns with the target market's needs.

8. **Scale the Business**: Establish partnerships or collaborations with other companies or organizations that can help with marketing, product development, or distribution channels. Implement marketing strategies to increase brand awareness and nurture customer relationships. Plan for product iterations, expansions, and support services to maintain a competitive edge in the industry.

In conclusion, AI-based emotion recognition technology offers promising business opportunities in 2024 due to its broad applicability across various industries. By carefully identifying market niches, assembling a strong team, securing funding, and ensuring compliance, entrepreneurs can seize this opportunity and create a successful and innovative start-up.

JAIME GEHLY

Smart Home Security Consultancy

In today's technologically advanced world, the concept of a smart home has gained significant popularity. However, as more homeowners adopt smart home technologies, concerns about privacy and cybersecurity have also grown. This presents an opportunity for a new and unique business venture: a Smart Home Security Consultancy.

The Smart Home Security Consultancy would specialize in helping homeowners secure their smart homes against cyber threats and privacy breaches. This venture is positioned for vast success given the current market landscape because it addresses a critical need in a rapidly expanding market while leveraging the growing awareness and demand for privacy and cybersecurity solutions.

Steps to Start the Business:

1. **Market Research**: Conduct thorough market research to identify the target audience, understand their pain points, and assess the competitive landscape. Analyze the current state of smart home security, industry trends, and emerging technologies.

2. **Define Services**: Develop a range of services that cater to the specific security needs of smart homes. This can include security audits, vulnerability assessments, network monitoring, device encryption, privacy policy reviews, and customized security solutions.

3. **Build Expertise**: Acquire the necessary knowledge and expertise in smart home security. This may involve obtaining relevant certifications, staying updated on industry best practices, and developing relationships with experts in cybersecurity and privacy.

4. **Strategic Partnerships**: Collaborate with manufacturers, smart home service providers, and technology vendors to offer integrated solutions and ensure compatibility with various smart home devices and systems. Forge partnerships with insurance companies to explore potential incentives or discounts for homeowners who implement recommended security measures.

5. **Marketing and Branding**: Develop a strong brand identity that reflects trust, expertise, and reliability. Create a comprehensive marketing strategy to raise awareness about the importance of smart home security and position the consultancy as a leader in the field. Utilize various channels such as digital

marketing, social media, and targeted advertising to reach the target audience effectively.

6. **Client Acquisition**: Implement a customer acquisition strategy that focuses on educating homeowners about the risks associated with smart home technologies and the value of investing in robust security measures. Offer free consultations or initial assessments to establish trust and demonstrate the expertise of the consultancy.

7. **Expand Network**: Attend industry conferences, trade shows, and networking events to build connections with potential clients, industry experts, and other stakeholders. Establish partnerships with home automation installers, home security companies, and real estate agents to expand the reach and referral network.

8. **Continuous Improvement**: Stay updated on the latest advancements in smart home technologies, cybersecurity, and privacy regulations. Continuously improve and evolve the service offerings to adapt to changing market needs and emerging threats.

The Smart Home Security Consultancy is a unique business venture positioned for success in the current market landscape. By addressing the growing concerns around smart home security and offering specialized services, this venture capitalizes on the expanding market while providing homeowners with peace of mind and protection for their smart homes. With a strategic approach, a strong brand, and a focus on expertise and customer satisfaction, this consultancy has the potential to thrive in the increasingly connected and security-conscious world.

JAIME GEHLY

Robotics for Agricultural Use

The agricultural sector has always played a crucial role in supporting the ever-growing global population. With the increasing need for higher crop yields, sustainable farm management, and reduced labor costs, a robotics start-up focused on agricultural applications in 2024 is poised for success. This paper outlines the reasons behind this potential and delineates the basic steps to get started with such a business venture.

Key Factors for Success:

1. **Technological Advancements**: The exponential development in robotics, AI, machine learning, and sensor technology will enable a start-up to create innovative, efficient, and cost-effective agricultural solutions.

2. **Demand for Precision Farming**: As global food demand continues to soar; farmers increasingly seek precision agriculture techniques that maximize yields and minimize resources. Robotics technology can help address this need through accurate monitoring, analyzing, and managing of crops and livestock.

3. **Labor Scarcity and Cost Reduction**: The agricultural sector faces a dearth of skilled labor and rising labor costs. Automating repetitive and labor-intensive tasks will not only save time and reduce costs but also improve worker safety.

4. **Sustainability**: Harnessing robotic solutions will enable eco-friendly practices such as optimized use of water, fertilizers, and pesticides. This aligns with the growing global demand for sustainable farming methods to reduce environmental impact.

5. **Government Support and Policy**: Governments worldwide have recognized the importance of agriculture and food security. Initiatives and funding schemes to support the development and adoption of advanced technologies in agriculture are proliferating, providing a conducive environment for start-ups to thrive.

Basic Steps to Get Started:

1. **Market Research and Analysis**: Thoroughly research and identify the niche within the agricultural robotics domain that offers the most potential based on market needs, competition, and opportunities.

2. **Develop a Business Plan**: Create a comprehensive plan outlining the business objectives, market strategy, revenue model, and operational structure. This will serve as a roadmap and provide direction.

3. **Assemble a Capable Team**: Form a multidisciplinary team of experts in robotics, AI, agriculture, software engineering, and marketing to build and promote the product effectively.

4. **Secure Funding**: Seek funding from angel investors, venture capitalists, grants, or government schemes. Demonstrating a clear business plan and product-market fit will increase the chances of obtaining financial backing.

5. **Research and Development**: Invest time and resources in designing, prototyping, and refining your agricultural robotic solution. Consult industry experts, collaborate with research institutions, and incorporate feedback from end-users to ensure maximum efficiency and usability.

6. **Obtain Necessary Permits and Certifications**: Acquire relevant permits, licenses, and certifications to ensure compliance with regulatory and safety requirements specific to the agricultural and robotics industries.

7. **Test and Validate Products**: Conduct rigorous on-field tests to validate product efficacy and performance under real-world conditions. Make adjustments as necessary before proceeding with mass production.

8. **Product Marketing and Sales Strategy**: Launch targeted marketing campaigns to create awareness and establish a market presence. Collaborate with local farming communities, agricultural associations, and distribution partners to increase visibility and sales of your robotics solutions.

9. **Continuous Improvement and Scaling Up**: Regularly assess market feedback, adapt to evolving industry trends, and enhance offerings. Aiming for a scalable business model will allow for growth and expansion within the agricultural landscape.

In summary, the urgency for sustainable and efficient agricultural practices, bolstered by rapid advances in robotics and AI, creates an unparalleled opportunity for a start-up business in agricultural robotics in 2024. By addressing critical needs and following the necessary steps, Agritech entrepreneurs stand to revolutionize an essential industry and contribute to a food-secure future.

Streamlined Home Renovation Solutions

The forecasted success of a streamlined home renovation solutions start-up in 2024 can be attributed to a growing demand globally for eco-friendly and energy-efficient housing, a surge in home sales due to favorable market conditions, an increased focus on remote and hybrid work setups, and technology advances that facilitate streamlined operations. By following basic steps such as conducting market research, drafting a solid business plan, identifying the target audience, utilizing technology, and offering customer-centered services, entrepreneurs in the home renovation industry can capitalize on these opportunities and achieve success in 2024.

In 2024, the global business landscape will continue to evolve, offering new opportunities for innovative entrepreneurs. One such opportunity is a streamlined home renovation solutions start-up focusing on eco-friendly, energy-efficient, and convenient housing solutions. Several factors contribute to the potential success of such a business, which align with growing market trends and technological developments.

Key Factors:

1. **Demand for Eco-Friendly and Energy-Efficient Housing**: Consumer preferences are increasingly shifting towards sustainable living, with a heightened demand for eco-friendly materials and energy-efficient technologies. By incorporating environmentally-friendly and energy-saving solutions into home renovations, the start-up will address these market demands effectively while reducing homeowners' costs and carbon footprints.

2. **Favorable Market Conditions**: Alongside rising homeownership rates, favorable market conditions like low-interest rates are bound to increase home sales in 2024. This surge presents a window of opportunity for home renovation businesses. Moreover, many homeowners will seek to upgrade their existing properties, creating a stable market for renovation services.

3. **Remote & Hybrid Work Setups**: The pandemic has accelerated the shift to more flexible work arrangements, with many companies adopting remote and hybrid work setups. As a result, homeowners are seeking functional, comfortable, and aesthetically-pleasing home offices. The home renovation start-up can capitalize on this trend by offering tailored renovation solutions for these spaces.

4. **Technology-Driven Streamlined Operations**: Technological innovations have created opportunities for streamlined operations and enhanced customer experience in the renovation industry. By using advanced tools like 3D modeling, virtual reality, and project management software, the start-up can offer clients a smooth and stress-free renovation experience.

Basic Steps to Get Started:

1. **Market Research**: Thoroughly investigate the local and global market trends and identify the primary business opportunities and challenges within the home renovation industry. Research the competition and study their strengths and weaknesses.

2. **Business Plan**: Draft a comprehensive business plan incorporating the start-up's goals, target demographics, budget, marketing strategy, and revenue projections. This plan will serve as a roadmap for the company and help attract investors.

3. **Target Audience**: Identify the target market segment, such as first-time homeowners, eco-conscious clients, or remote workers. This information will help tailor the start-up's services and marketing strategy accordingly.

4. **Technology and Innovation**: Embrace cutting-edge technology like 3D modeling, virtual reality, AI, and project management software to streamline the business and enhance customer experience.

5. **Customer-Centered Services**: Ensure that every project is completed with a focus on customer satisfaction. Adopt a transparent and efficient communication strategy to build trust and maintain long-term relationships with clients.

6. **Legal and Regulatory Requirements**: Obtain the necessary permits, licenses, and insurance coverage to operate legally within the renovation industry.

As the world continues to change in 2024, streamlined home renovation solutions will play a vital role in addressing these emerging needs. By focusing on eco-friendly solutions, embracing technology, and prioritizing customer satisfaction, a streamlined home renovation start-up will be primed for success in the coming years.

Privacy-Focused Messaging Apps and Services

The demand for privacy-focused messaging apps and services is skyrocketing in recent years due to increasing concerns regarding intrusions by governments, advertisers, and potential hackers. By 2024, a start-up in this domain is poised for success as the market continues its steady upward trajectory. This one-page summary aims to detail the reasons behind the projected success of a privacy-focused messaging and services start-up, as well as outline the basic steps required to launch this start-up.

Market Attraction:

1. **Increasing Public Awareness**: Data protection and privacy have become hot topics, with high-profile scandals like the Cambridge Analytica incident and the Edward Snowden revelations making headlines. This increases the demand for privacy-focused messaging apps and services, as users are becoming more aware of potential risks and want to protect their personal information.

2. **Legislative Developments**: The introduction of privacy-enhancing legislation in various regions, such as the European Union's General Data Protection Regulation (GDPR) and California's California Consumer Privacy Act (CCPA), demonstrates that countries are taking personal privacy more seriously. These developments create opportunities for a start-up offering compliance-focused products and services.

3. **Corporate Demand**: Remote work is becoming the norm, giving rise to the need for secure communication channels. Businesses are investing in adopting privacy-focused messaging apps and services to protect sensitive information and ensure secure communication when collaborating across distances.

4. **Competitive Landscape**: While existing market players such as WhatsApp, Signal, and Telegram have made strides in secure messaging, there is still room for innovative start-ups to differentiate themselves and capture niche segments.

101 BEST START-UP BUSINESS IDEAS FOR 2024 ACCORDING TO ADVANCED A.I.

Getting Started:

1. **Conceptualization and Market Research**: Identify the target market and specific requirements that the messaging application or service will address. Conduct thorough market research to understand the competition, product offerings, and customer pain points.

2. **Product Development**: Assemble a team of skilled security professionals and software engineers to develop a cutting-edge messaging platform with robust encryption, privacy features, and user-friendly interfaces. Incorporate feedback continuously during the development process.

3. **Legal and Regulatory Compliance**: Engage legal counsel to ensure the messaging app is compliant with relevant privacy regulations such as GDPR, HIPAA, and CCPA. Develop policies, such as terms of service and privacy policies, which clearly state data collection, storage, and usage practices.

4. **Building Partnerships**: Maximize the reach and market potential by partnering with relevant businesses and organizations. For instance, cooperate with companies involved in remote work, telecommunications, or cybersecurity industries.

5. **Marketing and Promotion**: Develop a marketing strategy that effectively informs the target audience about the start-up's differentiators, such as enhanced privacy and data protection capabilities. Utilize social media, blogs, industry events, and other channels to create awareness and generate excitement.

6. **Customer Support and Continuous Improvement**: Apart from providing a robust and user-friendly product, it is essential to offer excellent customer support to address user queries and concerns. Continually update the app based on user feedback and adopt new security features and privacy protocols as the industry evolves.

A privacy-focused messaging app and services start-up in 2024 is likely to experience significant commercial success due to increasing public awareness, legislative developments, and the rising demand for secure communication tools. By following the outlined steps and adhering to a strategic plan, the start-up will capitalize on this explosive demand and attract users who value privacy and data protection.

Voice Assistant Integration Services

The year 2024 marks a momentous time for the rise and proliferation of voice assistant technology. As consumers increasingly demand seamless, hands-free interactions with their smart devices, a voice assistant integration services start-up business stands poised to capitalize on this booming market. With collaboration, innovation, and a well-crafted strategy, such a start-up can successfully integrate voice assistance across various platforms and industries, ensuring convenience and efficiency for end-users.

Market Trends and Opportunities:

1. **Surging Demand for Voice Assistants**: With the rapid advancement of AI, voice assistant technology has become more sophisticated and reliable. As a result, the adoption rate of voice assistants like Google Assistant, Amazon's Alexa, and Apple's Siri has skyrocketed. Consumers are using these technologies at home, at work, and in their vehicles, showcasing the potential for a start-up to focus on integration services.

2. **The IoT Revolution**: The Internet of Things (IoT) is becoming an integral part of daily life, with an increasing number of smart devices entering the market. A voice assistant integration start-up can connect these devices to create seamless interconnections, improving user experience and generating increased demand for their services.

3. **Industry-Specific Applications**: Voice assistant integration presents opportunities for various industries, such as healthcare, finance, manufacturing, retail, and more. By offering industry-specific solutions, a start-up can target niche markets, solving unique challenges while differentiating themselves from competitors.

Steps to Launch a Voice Assistant Integration Services Start-up:

1. **Market Research**: Gain insights into the current voice assistant landscape, including potential competitors and niche markets. Identify opportunities and trends in the market that the start-up can capitalize on.

2. **Define Target Audience**: Determine the ideal customer base, including industries, individuals or businesses. Focusing on a niche target audience will allow efficient use of resources and cater to specific needs.

3. **Develop a Unique Value Proposition**: Focus on creating a unique value proposition that sets the start-up apart from competitors, highlighting the benefits of the integration services provided.

4. **Assemble a Core Team**: Build a skilled team, consisting of experts in AI, voice assistant technology, and business development. Collaboration between tech and business experts will ensure the start-up can deliver quality solutions while maintaining a clear overall vision.

5. **Establish Partnerships**: Forge strategic partnerships with voice assistant technology providers, IoT device manufacturers, and other industry stakeholders. These partnerships will provide better reach, increased credibility, and access to resources.

6. **Develop Integration Solutions**: Design and develop voice assistant integration solutions using state-of-the-art technology, prioritizing ease-of-use, flexibility, and scalability.

7. **Create a Marketing Strategy**: Develop a comprehensive marketing plan that promotes the start-up's unique voice assistant integration services across relevant platforms, including websites, social media, and industry events.

8. **Iterate and Optimize**: Continuously refine the integration services based on market feedback, to deliver an outstanding user experience and maintain competitive advantage.

A voice assistant integration services start-up, launched in 2024, is primed for success given the expanding adoption of voice assistants and the accelerating IoT revolution. By identifying niche markets, offering industry-specific solutions, and executing a well-rounded strategy, such a start-up can seize the opportunities offered by the thriving voice assistant landscape.

Lifestyle, Education, and Entertainment

AI-Generated Personalized Fashion

The fashion industry has long been known for its rapid pace of change and constant innovation. In the 21st century, the intersection of advanced technology and fashion has created a new market for personalized, AI-generated clothing. In this summary, we will discuss why an AI-generated personalized fashion start-up would be highly successful and profitable in 2024, as well as the basic steps required to get started with such a promising venture.

Reasons for Success and Profitability in 2024:

1. **Market Demand**: Consumers are increasingly favoring personalized experiences and products, especially when it comes to fashion. An AI-generated personalized fashion start-up would deliver on this growing demand, gaining considerable significance in an increasingly competitive market.

2. **Technological Advances**: Rapid advancements in AI and machine learning capabilities will enable accurate prediction of individual consumer preferences, based on user data such as browsing history, past purchases, and social interactions.

3. **Sustainable Fashion**: With the rise in environmental awareness, consumers are increasingly opting for sustainable clothing. AI-generated designs lead to less waste and more efficient manufacturing processes, helping create a brand image of environmentally-conscious fashion.

4. **Cost-Efficiency**: An AI-driven fashion start-up can efficiently manage a wide range of manufacturing processes, from fabric selection to garment assembly. Consequently, costs are reduced, driving profitability even further.

5. **Unique User Experience**: Implementing AI-generated fashion will create memorable user experiences, facilitate customization, and build customer loyalty, resulting in long-term profitability.

Steps to Get Started:

1. **Market Research**: Conduct thorough market research to understand the target audience, existing competition, and unexplored opportunities within the personalized fashion sector.

2. **Develop a Unique Value Proposition (UVP)**: Clearly outline your start-up's unique offering, focusing on the benefits of AI-generated personalized fashion in order to differentiate your brand from competitors.

3. **Assemble a Skilled Team**: Gather a team of talented professionals experienced in AI, machine learning, fashion, and marketing to successfully execute the start-up vision.

4. **Partner with Technology Providers** Identify and collaborate with reliable AI technology providers to develop specialized algorithms for predicting consumer preferences and generating unique designs.

5. **Establish Relationships with Manufacturers**: Partner with environmentally conscious manufacturers who can effectively and efficiently turn the personalized AI-generated designs into high-quality finished products.

6. **Develop a User-Friendly Website and App**: To ensure a seamless user experience, design an intuitive platform for customers to input preferences, view AI-generated designs, and order products.

7. **Launch a Marketing Plan**: Employ a strategic marketing plan to build brand awareness; leverage social media, influencer partnerships, and targeted ads to reach your target audience.

8. **Focus on Continuous Improvement**: Analyze customer feedback and market trends to improve designs, functionality, and overall features to stay relevant and competitive in a rapidly changing industry.

In conclusion, the future of fashion lies in delivering personalized experiences through advanced technologies like AI. With a unique value proposition, skilled team, and strategic execution, an AI-generated personalized fashion start-up is well-positioned for success and profitability in 2024.

JAIME GEHLY

Eco-Friendly Fashion Retail

In 2024, an eco-friendly fashion retail start-up business is poised to become a highly successful and profitable venture due to increasing consumer awareness, regulatory influences, and the potential for a sustainable, competitive market presence. By leveraging innovative business strategies and adhering to basic start-up principles, eco-friendly fashion retail start-ups can capitalize on these trends and build a thriving business.

Key Factors:

1. **Rising Consumer Awareness**: Sustainability has been a buzzword in the fashion industry for several years, and in 2024, it continues to be a top priority for consumers. As the public becomes even more environmentally conscious, demand for eco-friendly and ethically produced apparel is skyrocketing. People are now searching for sustainable products, prioritizing brands that are transparent about their supply chain, sourcing materials, and fair labor practices. Eco-friendly fashion retail start-ups can capitalize on this by promoting their ethical and sustainable manufacturing methods.

2. **Regulatory Influences**: Governments around the world are increasingly concerned about environmental sustainability, and this is having a direct impact on the fashion industry. New regulations are being implemented to encourage eco-friendly practices, such as incentivizing waste reduction, championing the circular economy, and promoting the use of renewable resources. As a result, having a business model built on sustainability will put an eco-friendly fashion retail start-up in an advantageous position to comply with these regulations and be recognized as a pioneer in the industry.

3. **Competitive Differentiator**: The eco-friendly fashion market represents a promising niche in the broader retail industry. By specializing in sustainable and ethical products, start-ups can differentiate themselves from competitors who follow traditional fast-fashion approaches. This differentiation not only attracts environmentally-aware customers but also allows the start-up to command higher price points for their sustainable materials and ethical production processes. As a result, the eco-friendly fashion retail business can generate higher profit margins and stand out in a crowded industry.

Steps to Start an Eco-Friendly Fashion Retail Business:

1. **Market Research and Business Planning**: Conduct in-depth market and customer research to understand target demographics, emerging trends, and possible competitors. Use this information to draft a comprehensive business plan that defines the business model, target market, and growth strategy.

2. **Sourcing Materials and Production Partners**: Carefully research and establish relationships with ethically responsible suppliers and manufacturers that share the same values and are committed to following sustainable practices.

3. **Branding and Marketing Strategy**: Create a strong brand identity rooted in eco-consciousness, and plan for an effective online and offline marketing strategy to spread awareness about the products, ethical values, and environmental impact.

4. **Establishing an Online Presence**: Develop an attractive and user-friendly website and leverage social media channels to engage with potential customers, promote products, and create a community of like-minded people.

5. **Invest in Sustainability Certifications**: Acquire necessary certifications and memberships to prove the brand's sustainable and ethical commitment, which reinforces consumer trust in the products.

6. **Retail Distribution and Pricing Strategy**: Choose the right retail distribution channels — either online, brick-and-mortar stores, or both– and set appropriate pricing to balance profitability and affordability for the target audience.

7. **Monitor Progress and Adapt**: Continuously assess performance, analyze customer feedback, and review industry trends to adapt and evolve the business strategy in a rapidly changing environmental and regulatory landscape.

In conclusion, an eco-friendly fashion retail start-up has immense scope for success and profitability in 2024 due to favorable consumer trends, regulatory pressures, and the appeal of a sustainable, differentiated market presence. With careful planning and a strong commitment to sustainability, such start-ups can thrive in an ever-evolving retail landscape.

Drone-Based Delivery Services

The rapid advancements in technology and changing consumer expectations have created an excellent opportunity for drone-based delivery services to thrive in 2024. These services offer numerous advantages, including reduced delivery times, cost-effectiveness, and enhanced sustainability. Starting a drone-based delivery service start-up can prove to be highly successful and profitable if properly planned and executed. This summary will outline the reasons behind this potential success and discuss the basic steps required to get started.

Market Opportunities:

1. **Increasing Online Shopping**: The growth of e-commerce has led to an increased demand for faster delivery options. Drones can significantly speed up delivery times compared to traditional methods, making them an attractive alternative for consumers and businesses.

2. **Demand for Contactless Delivery**: In the wake of the COVID-19 pandemic, contactless delivery has become increasingly important. Drone-based delivery services offer a safer and more hygienic way of delivering packages while minimizing human interaction.

3. **Environmental Sustainability**: Using drones for deliveries can reduce traffic congestion and CO_2 emissions, contributing to a greener and more sustainable world. This appeals to environmentally conscious consumers and businesses who prioritize sustainability in their decision-making.

Steps to Start a Drone-based Delivery Service Business:

1. **Market Research**: Conduct thorough market research to understand the potential demand for drone-based delivery services in the targeted region. This should include assessing the existing competition and identifying any untapped market opportunities.

2. **Develop a Business Plan**: Create a comprehensive business plan to outline the business's services, target market, marketing strategies, revenue generation models, and goals. The plan should be scalable and adaptive to various market changes.

3. **Legal and Regulatory Compliance**: Before starting operations, ensure compliance with local, regional, and national regulations. Obtain necessary

permits and licenses, and understand the restrictions and guidelines surrounding drone operations, such as flight paths, altitude limits, and no-fly zones.

4. **Procure Technology and Infrastructure**: Invest in cutting-edge drone technology, along with the required infrastructure, such as charging stations, drone maintenance facilities, and software systems for managing orders and logistical operations.

5. **Partner with Product Providers and Establish a Supply Chain**: Collaborate with e-commerce businesses, retailers, and local vendors to establish a supply chain network. Drone delivery services add value to their partners by reducing shipping time, lowering costs, and simplifying logistics.

6. **Build a Skilled Workforce**: Recruit and train skilled employees, including drone pilots, maintenance staff, and customer support representatives. Invest in employee development and well-being to foster a strong work environment.

7. **Pilot Testing and Market Launch**: Conduct comprehensive pilot tests to analyze the efficiency, cost-effectiveness, and customer satisfaction levels of the drone-based delivery system. Gather valuable user feedback and make any necessary adjustments before launching the services to the public.

8. **Build Brand Awareness and Marketing**: Develop a strong marketing campaign to reach potential customers and demonstrate the advantages of using drone-based delivery services. Utilize social media, local events, and partnerships to create a powerful brand identity and establish a reputation for quality service.

In conclusion, drone-based delivery services have immense potential to be successful and profitable in 2024. Taking advantage of growing market demands and technological advancements, these services can achieve high levels of customer satisfaction, improve efficiency, and contribute to a more sustainable future. By following the outlined steps, entrepreneurs can establish a successful drone-based delivery service start-up and capture a significant share of this growing market.

Premium Pet Care Services

The pet care industry has seen significant growth in recent years, and the future projections remain positive. A premium pet care services start-up in 2024 is poised to be highly successful and profitable. This start-up aims to provide top-quality services to pet owners who seek a convenient and personalized experience for their furry friends. With the pet humanization trend and increased pet ownership, a premium pet care services start-up would be a sustainable investment. To launch this business, identifying the target market, conducting extensive research, establishing a strong brand, and will be critical.

Market Demand:

In 2024, the pet care industry's growth will be fueled by the pet humanization trend and the continuously increasing number of pet owners. Pet owners consider their pets as family members and seek to provide them with the best possible care, products, and services. There is a clear market demand for premium pet care services, especially as pet owners became more conscious about the importance of high-quality care for their pets. This start-up's targeted customer base would comprise discerning pet owners who are willing to spend on top-tier services for their pets.

Steps to Get Started:

1. **Market Research**: Conduct comprehensive market research to understand the local pet care industry, potential competitors, and the customer base. This information will be invaluable for creating a business plan that effectively addresses the market demand for premium pet care services in 2024.

2. **Identify Target Market**: Define the ideal customer profile for the start-up, focusing on pet owners who prioritize the well-being of their pets and can afford high-quality care services. Market segmentation will help in creating effective marketing strategies.

3. **Create a Business Plan**: Develop a detailed business plan that outlines your vision, the services offered, pricing strategy, competitive analysis, marketing plan, and financial projections. This document will serve as a roadmap to launching and operating the premium pet care business.

4. **Establish a Brand Identity**: Position your start-up as a premium pet care services provider, focusing on exceptional quality, customer convenience, and

personalized care. Branding is critical in creating a distinctive identity that sets your start-up apart from competitors.

5. **Legalities and Permits**: Register your business and acquire any necessary licenses and permits to operate in your chosen location. Ensure compliance with local and federal regulations to avoid potential fines and penalties.

6. **Build a Team & Infrastructure**: Hire qualified and experienced professionals to deliver top-quality services. Invest in state-of-the-art pet care equipment and create a comfortable and clean environment to nurture a premium experience for the pets and their owners.

7. **Marketing and Promotion**: Craft a solid marketing strategy to build brand awareness and attract customers. Use a mix of traditional advertising, digital channels, social media, and local partnerships to garner interest in your premium pet care services.

8. **Monitor, Evaluate, and Adapt**: Regularly assess your start-up's performance and customer satisfaction. Be prepared to refine and expand your services based on changing customer needs and industry trends to maintain business success.

In 2024, a premium pet care services start-up has immense potential for profitability and success. By catering to the needs of pet owners who highly prioritize their pets' care, this start-up can capitalize on market demand, offering a convenient and personalized experience that resonates with customers. Following the steps detailed above can help lay the groundwork for a thriving and sustainable business in a booming industry.

JAIME GEHLY

Micro-Mobility Solutions

In 2024, the micro-mobility solutions start-up business is poised for high success and profitability due to its ability to cater to the intensified demand for efficient, eco-friendly, and flexible transportation systems. The rapidly growing urban population, escalating concerns over pollution levels and traffic congestion, and increasing environmental awareness among consumers are significant factors contributing to the promising market prospects. To launch a successful micro-mobility solutions start-up, entrepreneurs must devise a robust business plan, identify the target market, choose suitable micro-mobility vehicles and technology, acquire funding and permits, build a skilled team, and develop a strategic marketing campaign.

Key Factors for Success and Profitability in 2024:

1. **Increasing Urbanization**: With urban population growth rates continuously on the rise, the demand for efficient transportation to combat congestion and support the growing workforce is paramount. Micro-mobility solutions can contribute to smoother travel experiences, drastically reducing commute times and improving overall transportation efficiency.

2. **Eco-Friendly Solutions**: With mounting environmental concerns, lawmakers and consumers are seeking sustainable alternatives to curb pollution levels. Micro-mobility services using electric-powered vehicles such as e-scooters, bikes, and skateboards alleviate dependence on traditional, pollutant-emitting transportation methods, fostering air quality improvements.

3. **Health and Fitness Consciousness**: As health and fitness awareness rises, convenient and enjoyable options for incorporating physical activity into daily routines are sought after. Micro-mobility services distinctly support active transportation, promoting healthy lifestyles.

4. **Economical and Accessible**: Micro-mobility solutions answer both affordability and accessibility concerns. Appealing to a wide range of users, these services are generally affordable, enabling users to avoid costly investments in personal vehicles or traditional means of transportation.

Basic Steps to Get Started:

1. **Develop a Business Plan**: Carefully outline objectives, strategies, and tactics, addressing market research, target audience identification, vehicle type selection, pricing schemes, and revenue predictions. Analyze competitors, capitalize on trends, and address potential risks.

2. **Choose a Target Market**: Determine the market segment to engage, focusing on demographics, geography, and psychographics. Target markets might include tourists, urban commuters, college campuses, residential populations, or corporate communities.

3. **Select Micro-Mobility Vehicles and Technology**: Identify the vehicles best suited to cater to the target market and location, considering factors such as safety, efficiency, and maintenance requirements. Choose appropriate software and technology for fleet management, tracking, and user experience.

4. **Obtain Funding and Permits**: Garner support through crowdfunding, angel investors, venture capital firms, or government grants. Acquire local permits for fleet operations, safety requirements, and parking regulations.

5. **Assemble a Skilled Team**: Hire a skilled and experienced team, comprising experts in operations, customer service, maintenance, marketing, and sales departments. The team must collectively ensure smooth service delivery and a satisfying user experience.

6. **Develop a Marketing Campaign**: Design a strategic promotional campaign that resonates with the target market, leveraging both traditional and digital marketing channels. Engaging branding, user-friendly mobile apps, and catchy campaigns are essential in attracting and retaining users. Collaborate with local businesses or institutions to amplify visibility and credibility.

JAIME GEHLY

Personal Finance Management Apps

The global financial landscape is experiencing a paradigm shift in recent years, with technology and consumer needs aggressively revolutionizing the way individuals manage their finances. As a result, a personal finance management (PFM) apps start-up is poised to be highly successful and profitable in 2024. By offering user-friendly and comprehensive personal finance solutions, the start-up can capture a significant market share in this fast-growing industry. This summary delves into the reasons supporting this anticipated success and outlines the basic steps to establish a PFM start-up in 2024.

Reasons for Success:

1. **Increasing Need for Financial Organization**: As financial responsibilities grow more complex and global, consumers need better ways to categorize and manage income, expenses, investments, and debts. Streamlined PFM apps with AI-powered capabilities offer intuitive and customized solutions to cater to these demands.

2. **Expanding Financial Awareness**: PFM apps serve to enlighten users and foster healthy financial habits. An increased understanding of personal finance ultimately leads to better decision-making and improved long-term financial well-being.

3. **Ubiquity of Smartphone Usage**: With a rapidly increasing number of smartphone users worldwide, the potential consumer base for PFM apps is immense. As mobile technology further entrenches itself into everyday life, PFM apps become even more accessible, creating an unparalleled opportunity for growth.

4. **Data Security and Privacy**: As concerns over data privacy escalate, a PFM start-up that focuses on secure data handling, transparent practices, and stringent privacy measures will attract clients with heightened confidence.

5. **Customization and Scalability**: By employing advanced technologies such as machine learning and AI, PFM apps can provide personalized financial insights and advice. As a result, the apps remain relevant and valuable to users throughout various life stages and financial situations.

Steps to Get Started:

1. **Market Research**: Conduct in-depth market research to understand consumer needs, preferences, pain points, and purchasing behavior. Identify target market segments, study competitors, and evaluate the potential for growth and profitability.

2. **App Conceptualization**: Based on the research, conceptualize a PFM app that addresses identified market gaps, resonates with the target audience, and sets the start-up apart from the competition.

3. **MVP (Minimum Viable Product) Development**: Develop a PFM app MVP with essential features, focusing on user experience (UX) and user interface (UI) design. This MVP will serve as a foundation for testing, feedback, and future iterations.

4. **Data Security and Compliance**: Invest in state-of-the-art security measures to safeguard user data and ensure compliance with applicable data protection regulations.

5. **Establish a Marketing Strategy**: Develop a comprehensive marketing strategy that includes market positioning, brand identity, and promotional campaigns. Leverage digital marketing channels, social media, content, and strategic partnerships to generate awareness and user acquisition.

6. **Funding and Finances**: Secure early-stage investments from angel investors, VCs, or crowdfunding platforms to fund app development, marketing, and operation.

7. **Launch, Analyze, and Iterate**: Launch the app in a phased manner to test its viability and gather user feedback. Monitor key performance indicators (KPIs) and continuously iterate the app to improve engagement, user satisfaction, and monetization.

With increasing financial awareness, the ubiquity of smartphone usage, conscientious utilization of data security, and a focus on customization and scalability, a personal finance management app start-up has the potential for immense success in 2024. By following these fundamental steps, entrepreneurs can seize this opportunity and create a formidable and profitable presence in the PFM industry.

Travel Planning and Booking Platform

In 2024, launching a travel planning and booking platform start-up business is poised to be highly successful and profitable, thanks to various factors that drive the travel industry's growth. Moreover, innovations in technology present a unique opportunity for entrepreneurs to cater to the market's evolving demands. This brief summary outlines the reasons behind this potential success and details the steps a prospective start-up should take to get started in the travel planning and booking sector.

Why a Highly Successful and Profitable Business?

1. **Post-Pandemic Travel Boom**: As restrictions imposed during the COVID-19 pandemic are lifted, the pent-up demand for travel creates a surge in bookings, driving revenue for travel-related businesses.

2. **Shift in Trends**: In 2024, travelers show an increased preference for personalized and authentic experiences. This creates opportunities for a travel planning and booking platform to cater to their needs through curated travel plans and services.

3. **Technology Adoption**: The extensive use of smartphones and Internet connectivity drive the adoption of digital platforms for all aspects of travel planning and booking in this era.

4. **Demographic Factors**: Millennials and Gen Z consumers, who are tech-savvy and prioritize experiences over material possessions, are key customers for the travel industry.

5. **Sustainable Travel**: Growing awareness of climate change and the necessity of sustainable practices offers opportunities for eco-conscious start-ups to make inroads in this market.

Basic Steps to Get Started:

1. **Market Research**: Conduct comprehensive market research to identify unique selling propositions, target segments, and competition. Use the findings to devise a distinct and appealing value proposition that will stand out in the market.

2. **Business Model**: Choose an appropriate business model that addresses the needs and preferences of the target audience. Consider models like online marketplaces, affiliate platforms, or commissions on bookings.

3. **Platform Development**: Develop a user-friendly platform (website and mobile application) focusing on user experience and easy navigation. Implement advanced search features, personalized recommendations, AI-driven customer assistance, and secure payment options.

4. **Establishing Strong Partnerships**: Partner with various travel service providers like hotels, airlines, car rental agencies, tour operators, and insurance companies to enable customers to access a range of services from a single platform.

5. **Compliance and Licensing**: Establish legal compliance and obtain the necessary licenses and permits for operating in the business's target jurisdiction.

6. **Marketing Strategy**: Craft a marketing strategy that appeals to the target audience. opt for social media marketing, content marketing, search engine optimization (SEO), and influencer marketing to create brand awareness and drive website traffic.

7. **Fundraising**: Secure funding for the start-up through venture capital, angel investors, or crowdfunding campaigns.

8. **Test the Platform**: Prior to launching, test the platform with a select group of users and gather their feedback to refine and optimize the system.

By harnessing the innovative potential of technology, a travel planning and booking platform start-up in 2024 is poised to achieve high levels of success and profitability, meeting the evolving demands of a travel-hungry market.

JAIME GEHLY

Online Maker Spaces for Craftsmen

In 2024, the market landscape for a successful online maker space for craftsmen start-up business will be highly profitable, thanks to the combination of increased interest in online commerce, the growing appreciation for artisanal products, and the advancement of technologies facilitating the integration of crafts into the digital world. The following points outline the favorable conditions for the start-up and the basic steps required for its inception.

Key Points Supporting Success and Profitability:

1. **Growing E-Commerce Landscape**: As the world increasingly adopts online commerce, new businesses aiming to provide a virtual space for craftsmen will thrive in the market. The projected growth of e-commerce in the coming years presents greater opportunities for creators and artists to generate significant revenue.

2. **Appreciation for Handcrafted Goods**: Consumers are becoming more conscious of the importance of local and handcrafted products. The demand for unique, high-quality artisanal goods is on the rise, as people seek authentic alternatives to mass-produced items. This trend leads to a significant potential for profitability in the crafts sector.

3. **Technological Advancements**: The rapid evolution of technology has opened avenues for integrating artisanal crafts into the digital world. The development of virtual and augmented reality platforms allows online showcases and interactive workshops, enabling artisans to connect with their audience and expand their reach in ways never before possible.

4. **Environmental Focus**: With the growing emphasis on sustainability and eco-friendliness, consumers are embracing handcrafted products that offer a low environmental footprint compared to mass-produced options. By focusing on products that contribute positively to the environment, an online maker space for craftsmen start-up business is positioned to gain considerable customer loyalty and support.

101 BEST START-UP BUSINESS IDEAS FOR 2024 ACCORDING TO ADVANCED A.I.

Basic Steps to Get Started:

1. **Define the Business Concept**: Determine the niche of the business, whether it is an online marketplace, platform for online classes, or a collaboration network for craftsmen. Be specific and outline how the start-up will serve artisans and their customers in a unique, valuable way.

2. **Perform Market Research**: Conduct thorough market research to identify your target audience, competition, and potential collaborators. Analyze the data to remain informed on the latest trends and gaps in the market, and establish a suitable business direction.

3. **Develop a Business Plan**: Create a comprehensive business plan that includes the company's mission, objectives, marketing strategies, and financial projections. The business plan will serve as a road map and foundation for your start-up.

4. **Register the Business**: Choose a suitable legal structure and register the business with the appropriate government agencies. Take care of essential processes such as obtaining relevant permits and licenses, as well as securing liability insurance, when necessary.

5. **Build a Web Platform**: Develop an engaging and easy-to-use online platform for your maker space. Collaborate with experienced web developers and designers to create the website or mobile application, ensuring it reflects your brand image and appeals to your target audience.

6. **Marketing and Promotion**: Utilize a range of digital marketing techniques, such as social media, content marketing, and email campaigns, to promote the platform to craftsmen and customers. Engage with your audience through informative and creative content that highlights your unique offerings.

An online maker space for craftsmen start-up business in 2024 has tremendous potential for success and profitability. By following these basic steps and taking advantage of the favorable market conditions, entrepreneurs can create a thriving and sustainable platform that bridges the gap between traditional and digital, and supports the growth of craftsmanship in the digital age.

Adaptive E-Learning Platforms

Adaptive e-learning platforms have emerged as a highly successful and profitable start-up option in the ever-evolving education technology sector. Rapid advancements in technology, increased internet access, and growing demand for personalized and flexible learning approaches have all contributed to this phenomenon. To launch a thriving adaptive e-learning platform start-up in 2024, an entrepreneur must focus on understanding the market, developing a scalable and innovative product, building strong partnerships, and implementing a robust marketing strategy.

Market Need:

By 2024, the need for personalized learning experiences catering to unique learning styles is more evident than ever. Traditional learning methods are being replaced by advanced digital solutions, as students and professionals alike seek better ways to acquire new skills and knowledge. Adaptive e-learning platforms effectively bridge this gap by leveraging cutting-edge technology to deliver an immersive learning experience on-demand, making them well-positioned for success in the 21st century.

Key Factors for Success:

1. **Understanding the Market**: Conduct in-depth research to identify target demographics and their specific needs. Assess current trends, potential competitors, and market gaps to find unique selling propositions.

2. **Consumer-Centric Product Design**: Develop an adaptive e-learning platform with user-friendly interfaces and features that cater to diverse learning needs. Incorporate artificial intelligence (AI) and machine learning systems that understand learners' abilities, preferences, and progress to deliver tailored content accordingly.

3. **Engaging Content Creation**: Collaborate with subject matter experts to create high-quality, up-to-date, and relevant learning materials. Focus on developing engaging content formats, such as interactive videos, simulations, quizzes, and gamification elements for an immersive learning experience.

4. **Scalable Product Architecture**: Work on a robust technical infrastructure to handle high user loads and provide seamless access to resources. Prioritize scalability and security to accommodate rapid growth and ensure that your

adaptive e-learning platform meets evolving legal and data security requirements.

5. **Partnerships**: Forge partnerships with educational institutions, corporations, and industry experts to stay ahead of the curve, expand your content library, and drive more enrollments.

6. **Continuous Improvement**: Enhance your platform by regularly analyzing user feedback, monitoring performance metrics, and implementing improvements. This agile approach will help you stay ahead of the competition and meet the changing needs of learners.

7. **Effective Marketing and Sales Strategy**: Develop a strategic marketing plan to raise awareness and generate interest in your platform. Utilize data-driven marketing channels like search engine optimization (SEO), social media marketing, email marketing, and content marketing to reach your target audience. Implement sales strategies, pricing models, and promotional activities to increase enrollments and improve customer retention.

Adaptive e-learning platform start-ups have tremendous growth potential in 2024 and beyond, provided entrepreneurs understand the contexts in which they operate and the key steps necessary to launch a thriving venture. By addressing learners' diverse needs through personalized and flexible learning solutions, entrepreneurs in this field will not only build a highly successful and profitable business, but also contribute significantly to the global educational landscape.

Socially-Conscious Artisan Marketplaces

As we enter the year 2024, the vision of a socially-conscious artisan marketplace startup aligns not only with the increasing global awareness of socio-environmental challenges but also with the changing consumer needs and priorities. With an innovative, sustainable, and ethical business model at its core, a socially-conscious artisan marketplace has the potential to achieve tremendous success and profitability. The following factors and steps are crucial in achieving this success in today's economy.

Demographic Shift: There has been a significant shift in the demographic landscape, especially with the growing influence of millennials and Generation Z, who are now the most significant cohorts driving consumer behavior. These generations are mindful of their consumption patterns and are actively seeking environmentally responsible options, placing a high value on transparency, ethical sourcing, fair trade practices, and social impact initiatives.

Consumer Trends: As we progress further into the digital age, society continues to see an increase in environmental awareness, ethical consumerism, and demand for personalized experiences. A socially-conscious artisan marketplace that curates products from various ethical and sustainable brands, ensuring a low environmental footprint and fair working conditions, caters directly to the heart of these consumer trends.

Global Demand for Sustainable Products:

Nowadays, people have become more environmentally conscious and are looking for alternative products that don't contribute to environmental degradation. Additionally, there is growing importance for local economies, seeking ways to support small and medium-sized enterprises (SMEs) and artisans. By connecting consumers with artisans' handcrafted and sustainable products, these marketplaces contribute to the growth of responsible consumerism and bolster local economies.

Steps to Get Started:

1. **Define the Vision and Mission**: A strong vision and mission will guide the startup in aligning its values, objectives, branding, and messaging throughout every phase of business development.

2. **Conduct Market Research**: Research market trends and competitors, identify the target market, and determine the most pressing needs of your potential customers.

3. **Develop a Business Model**: Create a sustainable and innovative business model that includes a unique value proposition and an ethical supply chain, ensuring ethical sourcing and fair-trade practices.

4. **Secure Funding**: Prepare a compelling business plan, financial forecast, and pitch deck to attract investors or secure funding through alternative means such as grants, crowdfunding, or loans.

5. **Build a strong online presence**: Design and develop a user-friendly, intuitive platform that allows artisans to set up their digital storefronts and connect with customers, ensuring ease of navigation and a seamless user experience.

6. **Onboard Artisans**: Establish a robust vetting process to attract, authenticate, and onboard only those artisans who abide by the marketplace's ethical and sustainability guidelines.

7. **Marketing and Brand Positioning**: Develop and implement effective marketing and branding strategies, such as content marketing, social media campaigns, and influencer collaborations, to create positive brand awareness and amplify the platform's socially conscious message.

8. **Optimize and Analyze**: Continuously collect data, analyze metrics, and optimize the platform and business model to meet the changing market demands and facilitate growth.

By capitalizing on the growing environmentally-conscious consumer base, promoting local economies and sustainability, and by offering a user-friendly, ethical shopping platform, a socially-conscious artisan marketplace start-up has the potential to become a highly successful and profitable business in 2024.

JAIME GEHLY

Ethical Cosmetics: Cruelty-Free and Eco-Friendly

In the upcoming year 2024, an ethical cosmetics start-up focusing on cruelty-free and eco-friendly products is primed for significant success and profitability. This can be attributed to the growing awareness of animal rights and environmental sustainability, and the subsequent shift in consumer preferences. In this summary, we will delve into the reasons behind this potential success and outline the essential steps required to launch such a start-up.

Market Trends and Opportunities:

1. **Consumer Demand**: Increasing awareness of environmental issues and animal rights has led to a higher demand for ethical cosmetics products. As more consumers seek sustainable, cruelty-free products, businesses that adhere to these practices are set to reap the benefits.

2. **Market Growth**: The ethical cosmetics market has been consistently growing, with a projected CAGR of about 6.5% from 2021 to 2028. This presents a significant opportunity for new entrants into the market.

3. **Competitive Advantage**: Focusing on ethical cosmetics allows businesses to differentiate themselves from competitors and establish a strong, loyal customer base. Offering transparency in sourcing and production methods can further boost the brand's reputation.

4. **Regulatory Environment**: The global push towards banning animal testing in cosmetics and increased regulations favor eco-friendly businesses, providing ethical cosmetics start-ups with a promising future.

Basic Steps to Get Started:

1. **Research**: Conduct market research to understand customer preferences, competitors, and niche opportunities in the ethical cosmetics industry. This will help guide product development and branding strategies.

2. **Business Planning**: Develop a comprehensive business plan, including financial projections, a well-defined target market, and a marketing strategy. This plan will serve as the foundation for your start-up and attract potential investors.

3. **Product Development**: Create high-quality, cruelty-free, and eco-friendly cosmetic products that adhere to industry standards and regulations. Collaborate with labs or chemists to ensure that your formulations are innovative, safe, and effective.

4. **Sourcing and Suppliers**: Establish relationships with ethical suppliers who can provide cruelty-free, sustainable raw materials and packaging. This crucial aspect of the business impacts the brand's overall image and sustainability goals.

5. **Branding and Marketing**: Develop a strong brand identity and marketing strategy that emphasizes the ethical and eco-friendly aspect of the company. Utilize social media, influencer marketing, and targeted advertising to create awareness and appeal to your target customer base.

6. **Sales Channels**: Decide on the most suitable sales channels for your products, such as direct-to-consumer through an eCommerce website, retail partnerships, or both.

7. **Legalities and Regulations**: Ensure compliance with local and international regulations pertaining to cosmetics, animal testing, and environmental standards. Consider trademarks, copyrights, and other intellectual property protection.

8. **Funding**: Secure investments, loans, or grants to finance your start-up. Explore the possibility of partnerships or collaboration with established ethical cosmetics brands or investors interested in sustainable and cruelty-free products.

In 2024, an ethical cosmetics start-up, focusing on cruelty-free and eco-friendly products, has the potential to achieve significant success and profitability. Seizing opportunities presented by the growing market and public awareness of sustainability, and adhering to the basic steps required to establish the business are essential to realizing this potential.

Esports Coaching Platforms

Esports has experienced tremendous growth in recent years, with forecasts estimating the global esports market to reach USD 1.79 billion in revenue by the end of 2024. An esports coaching platform start-up business has the potential to capitalize on this trend and offers a lucrative opportunity for investors and entrepreneurs. This summary outlines the reasons for this promising venture and provides a step-by-step guide to getting started.

Growing Market Potential:

1. **Emergence of Esports**: Esports has solidified itself as a mainstream form of entertainment, further supported by the ongoing success of major gaming tournaments, celebrity endorsements, and an increasing number of dedicated esports arenas. These factors contribute to a thriving ecosystem that would be welcoming to an esports coaching platform start-up.

2. **Increase in Consumer Demand**: The popularity of esports has also led to a growth in amateur players seeking to hone their skills and compete at higher levels. An esports coaching platform catering to this demand would provide a valuable service to a wide range of gamers.

3. **Attractive Target Demographic**: Esports primarily attracts a young and technologically-savvy audience. This demographic is open to innovative solutions and is more likely to engage with a coaching platform for skill improvement and training.

Steps to Get Started:

1. **Market Research**: Conduct comprehensive market research to understand the scope and potential of the esports industry, and identify the most popular games and genres. This research will help in determining potential target audiences and designing appropriate services.

2. **Define Business Model and Services**: Develop a clear business model and outline the coaching platform's services. Services may include personalized coaching, video tutorials, live workshops, game analytics, and performance monitoring. Consider offering tiered pricing, starting with a basic package and moving up to more advanced or premium options.

3. **Legal and Regulatory Compliance**: Obtain licenses and register the start-up company, ensuring the business adheres to legal requirements in the relevant jurisdiction. Research any specific esports-related regulations, permits, or approvals that may be needed.

4. **Platform Development and Technology**: Create an accessible and user-friendly platform that supports various devices (PC, consoles, mobile). Integrate AI-driven analytics, communication tools, and other features to enhance user experience and facilitate a more personalized learning process.

5. **Assemble a Team of Coaches**: Recruit experienced esports coaches with a proven track record for competitive play and coaching in their respective games. Ensure the coaches are well-versed in both game mechanics and teaching methods.

6. **Marketing and Promotion**: Develop a marketing strategy tailored to your target audience, which may include content marketing, social media advertising, influencer partnerships, and sponsorships. Leverage the popularity of esports players, teams, and tournaments to create buzz around the platform.

7. **Launch and Monitor Performance**: Launch the platform, while continuously monitoring user engagement and platform performance. Be prepared to pivot or adapt offerings in response to user feedback, industry trends, or changes in the competitive landscape.

In 2024, an esports coaching platform start-up business represents an exciting and potentially lucrative venture. With consistent market growth, increasing consumer demand, and a willing audience, entrepreneurs can take advantage of this opportunity by providing valuable services to amateurs and professional gamers alike. Following the outlined steps, business owners can create a successful platform and become a valuable asset to the ever-growing esports community.

JAIME GEHLY

Plant-Based Meat Alternatives

The rapidly increasing consumer demand for sustainable and healthy food options, coupled with the global environmental concerns, make a plant-based meat alternatives start-up business an excellent venture for entrepreneurs in 2024. This document provides a summary of the reasons behind the potential success of such business and outlines the basic steps required to get started.

Reasons for Success:

1. **Rising Demand for Plant-Based Alternatives**:

In recent years, there has been a dramatic rise in the popularity of plant-based meat alternatives, driven primarily by health-conscious consumers and environmental sustainability advocates. This trend is expected to continue, making plant-based meat alternatives a lucrative market.

2. **Health Benefits**:

Research has shown that plant-based diets have several health benefits, such as lower risks for heart disease, diabetes, and obesity, which are major global health concerns. This positions plant-based meat alternatives as attractive and advantageous to health-conscious consumers.

3. **Climate Change Mitigation**:

The production of traditional meat products is associated with high carbon emissions, deforestation, and excessive water usage. With plant-based meat alternatives being a more sustainable option, their adoption may contribute significantly to climate change mitigation and help avert environmental crises.

4. **Market Expansion**:

Since the plant-based meat alternatives market is relatively young, there is considerable room for expansion and innovation. A start-up in this space can take advantage of the opportunities presented by the evolving market to create innovative and appealing products that cater to changing consumer tastes.

Basic Steps to Get Started:

1. **Market Research**: Begin by conducting thorough market research to gain insight into consumer preferences, trends, and competitive landscape. Identify the plant-based meat alternative products that are most favored or are currently lacking in the market.

2. **Product Development**: Create a unique product line that caters to your target market by focusing on taste, texture, and nutritional value. Consider leveraging innovative food technologies, such as fermentation, extrusion, and plant proteins, that enable the creation of high-quality plant-based meat alternatives.

3. **Brand Development and Identity**: Establish a strong brand identity that resonates with your target market and conveys your product's unique selling proposition. Make sure your branding highlights aspects like taste, health benefits, and environmental sustainability.

4. **Financial Planning and Funding**: Develop a comprehensive business plan detailing financial projections, start-up costs, and revenue streams. Seek funding through various channels, including bank loans, personal savings, investors, or crowd-funding platforms.

5. **Regulatory Compliance and Certifications**: Ensure compliance with food safety regulations and acquire necessary permits and certifications, such as USDA organic, non-GMO, or vegan-certified labels.

6. **Production and Distribution**: Establish your production facility, either by setting up your own manufacturing unit or partnering with co-packers. Develop a robust distribution network that includes wholesalers, retailers, and online sales channels to make your products easily accessible to your target market.

7. **Marketing and Promotion**: Implement a comprehensive marketing strategy to create brand awareness and generate consumer interest. Utilize various marketing channels such as social media, print media, and influencer partnerships. Participate in industry events, trade shows, and product tastings to showcase your products and grow your consumer base.

By seizing the opportunities presented by consumer demand, health benefits, climate change mitigation, and market expansion, a plant-based meat alternatives start-up in 2024 has the potential to be an incredibly successful venture. Proper planning, execution, and adaptation based on continuous market analysis will be the keys to success for entrepreneurs stepping into this space.

JAIME GEHLY

Remote Team Collaboration Tools

In today's rapidly evolving digital landscape, several factors contribute to transforming a start-up business into a money-making venture. As the year 2024 approaches, the demand for proficient, user-friendly remote team collaboration tools is skyrocketing. Employers and their teams are embracing the benefits of remote work, creating a lucrative market for any start-up that can cleverly address the potential challenges of distributed workforces.

Market Potential:

The remote work trend has become increasingly prevalent owing to advancements in digital infrastructure and a paradigm shift in people's approach to work. A significant number of companies around the globe are opting for, or at least considering, remote work policies to generate cost savings, improve work-life balance and ensure continued operations during disruptive times. This means the market for collaboration tools is vast and ripe for the taking, with opportunities to cater to businesses of all sizes.

Benefits of Remote Collaboration Tools:

Investing in a remote collaboration tools start-up in 2024 promises substantial financial returns, as the need for increased productivity, reduced miscommunication, and better time and resource management becomes more apparent. Efficient remote collaboration tools can enable employees to collaborate in real-time, host virtual meetings, share files and documents, and communicate seamlessly across different time zones. This allows companies to maximize their global talent pool and optimize operations without adding to their overhead costs.

Basic Steps to Get Started:

1. **Research and Ideation**: Begin by researching the remote collaboration tools market, identifying the key players and noting their strengths and weaknesses. Understand the needs of potential businesses and identify any gaps in the current offerings. Develop an innovative technological solution that addresses these requirements while offering a unique advantage.

2. **Develop a Business Model**: Create a sustainable business model outlining the value proposition, target market, revenue streams, and service offerings. Also,

develop a distinctive marketing strategy that differentiates your product from competitors.

3. **Assemble a Strong Team**: Form a team of motivated and talented individuals with experience in software development, design, business management, and marketing. This will ensure that all areas of the start-up are in capable hands.

4. **Secure Funding**: Seek initial funding through sources like angel investors, venture capitalists, or personal financing. Provide a comprehensive pitch that showcases how your start-up will disrupt the market and generate steady revenues.

5. **Develop the Collaboration Tool**: With a carefully designed product roadmap and developmental milestones in place, kick-start your software development process. Ensure your remote collaboration tool is not only functional but also user-friendly and visually appealing. Identify the essential features, such as file sharing, real-time communication, and project management, and prioritize their development to create a minimum viable product (MVP).

6. **Beta Testing and Iterations**: Launch your collaboration tool to a limited audience for testing and gather their feedback. Iterate and improve your product to address any issues or gaps, then optimize the tool based on this feedback.

7. **Marketing and Launch**: Develop and execute a strategic marketing campaign to attract potential users and encourage business adoption. Utilize digital marketing channels such as social media, email marketing, SEO, and content creation to target your audience effectively.

In summary, a remote team collaboration tools start-up business in 2024 offers vast potential for financial success as businesses recognize the advantages of remote work. With proper planning and execution, a responsive and valuable remote collaboration tool can secure strong market positioning and consistently generate revenue.

Sleep Optimization Solutions

The current fast-paced society and increased technological dependency have resulted in a high prevalence of sleep disorders and inadequate sleep quality. A sleep optimization solutions start-up business in 2024 presents a unique opportunity to capitalize on the growing market demand for products and services that improve sleep quality, ultimately leading to enhanced physical and mental well-being. This document will outline the factors that make such a start-up an attractive money-maker in 2024 and the essential steps to kick-start the venture.

Market Drivers:

1. **Increasing Prevalence of Sleep Disorders**: Sleep disorders, such as insomnia and sleep apnea, are on the rise due to various factors such as demanding work lives, increased screen time, and aging populations. These rising numbers indicate the need for effective and reliable sleep solutions, creating a promising market for a start-up.

2. **Stress and Anxiety Escalation**: The uncertainty of modern living and an increasingly interconnected world have resulted in higher stress and anxiety levels. Consequently, people are actively seeking alternative methods to improve their sleep and overall well-being.

3. **Rise in Remote Working**: Owing to the COVID-19 pandemic, remote working has become more prevalent, altering people's daily routines and sleep patterns. This shift in lifestyle leads to additional demand for sleep optimization tools to help professionals maintain their productivity and well-being.

4. **Technological Advances**: Cutting-edge technologies, such as artificial intelligence, biofeedback, and wearable devices, are experiencing rapid advancements. These technologies can be used to create tailored sleep optimization solutions, drawing the attention of investors and customers alike.

Basic Steps to Get Started:

1. **Market Research**: Thorough research into the sleep solutions market is crucial to identify the prevalent trends, competitors, and potential customers. This information will inform the start-up's business model and product development.

2. **Developing a Unique Product or Service**: Develop a unique offering by leveraging advancements in technology or innovative approaches to sleep optimization. This could include developing a device or software, providing consulting services, or creating a content platform.

3. **Creating a Business Plan**: Draft a comprehensive business plan that details the company's mission, target market, marketing strategies, financial projections, and operational structure.

4. **Securing Funding**: Acquire the necessary funds through various means, such as venture capital, angel investment, crowdfunding, or personal savings. This capital will be used in product development, team recruitment, and other initial expenses.

5. **Building a Qualified Team**: Assemble a skilled team drawn from various fields, including sleep science, software development, marketing, and healthcare, to bring the product or service to life and promote its growth.

6. **Launching a Minimum Viable Product (MVP)**: Develop and release an MVP to gather user feedback and market insights on the product or service's performance. The iterative process allows for improvement based on this feedback, leading to a refined and more efficient offering.

7. **Marketing**: Establish a strong presence through social media platforms, content marketing, online and offline promotional campaigns, and strategic partnerships to promote the start-up to target audiences.

By identifying market trends and capitalizing on emerging technologies, a sleep optimization solutions start-up in 2024 presents a highly lucrative business opportunity. Careful planning, product development, and execution can create a lasting impact on improving people's lives while generating considerable revenue.

Space Tourism

With the rapid advancements in technology and increased public interest in space travel, launching a space tourism start-up is poised for tremendous success in 2024. The market potential, technological advancements, and numerous strategic partnerships will drive its growth, making it an attractive business venture.

Demand for Space Tourism: The demand for space tourism has reached new heights, with more people interested in experiencing microgravity and observing Earth from space. There is a market for both suborbital and long-stay orbital experiences. The increasing number of high-net-worth individuals willing to pay a premium for a unique and once-in-a-lifetime trip demonstrates potential for exponential growth in this sector.

Technological Advancements: Recent years have seen an immense acceleration in the development of spaceflight technologies. Reusable rockets, propulsion systems, and private companies like SpaceX, Blue Origin, and Virgin Galactic have advanced rapidly. Their successes have reduced costs and increased both safety and reliability, making space tourism a viable option for a broader range of customers.

Government Involvement: Countries around the world are eager to participate and invest in space tourism, recognizing its potential economic impact. Governments are offering incentives, subsidies, and other support for the development of commercial space ventures. This involvement eases the regulatory and financial burdens for start-ups and stimulates market competition.

Strategic Partnerships: A successful space tourism start-up in 2024 will leverage strategic partnerships with key stakeholders from various industries, including technology, aerospace, insurance, and hospitality. Combining resources and expertise will result in an innovative tourism product that capitalizes on market potential, enhances customer experience, and ensures safety.

Basic Steps to Start a Space Tourism Venture:

1. **Market Research**: Conduct comprehensive market research to identify target segments, understand their preferences, evaluate competitors, and determine potential risks and opportunities in the industry.

2. **Develop a Business Plan**: Define the mission, vision, and goal of the start-up. Address key elements like funding, organizational structure, customer experience, pricing strategy, and regulatory requirements. An effective business plan is essential for attracting investors and partners.

3. **Acquire Necessary Funding**: Identify various funding sources such as angel investors, venture capital firms, and government grants. Present your business plan to secure the funds necessary for research, development, testing, and marketing efforts.

4. **Build an Expert Team**: Assemble a group of professionals with experience and expertise in space technology, aviation, aerospace engineering, marketing, and related fields. This team will drive the success of the start-up by addressing technical challenges and promoting the vision.

5. **Develop the Technology**: Partner with aerospace technology companies, or develop in-house capabilities to design, produce, and operate spacecraft necessary for your space tourism business. Focus on safety, affordability, and sustainability.

6. **Ensure Regulatory Compliance**: Work closely with regulatory authorities like the Federal Aviation Administration (FAA) and other international organizations to obtain proper permits, licensing, and certification.

7. **Prioritize Safety and Training**: Invest in rigorous flight crew training and passenger safety orientation to minimize risks and ensure the highest safety standards.

8. **Marketing and Promotion**: Establish a powerful brand identity and promote it using digital and traditional media, events, influencers, and public relations. Attract customers by emphasizing the unique and innovative aspects of the space travel experience.

In conclusion, 2024 is the perfect time for a space tourism start-up to thrive. Capitalizing on the growing demand, technological advances, and supportive governments will pave the way for a hugely successful business venture.

JAIME GEHLY

Lab-Grown Meat Production

In recent years, the world has become increasingly aware of the environmental, ethical, and health implications associated with traditional animal agriculture. As a result, the demand for alternative protein sources has surged. One of the most promising solutions is lab-grown meat, also known as cultured or cell-based meat. In 2024, starting a lab-grown meat production business is a smart decision due to the escalating market demand, favorable policies and regulations, emerging technology, and business opportunities. This summary outlines the reasons for launching a lab-grown meat production start-up and the basic steps required to get started.

Key Factors:

1. **Market Potential**: The global market for lab-grown meat is projected to grow exponentially in the coming years. With rising concerns over environmental sustainability, animal welfare, and the efficiency of traditional meat production methods, consumers are seeking ethical and sustainable alternatives. This consumer trend is likely to make lab-grown meat a sought-after product in the near future, creating a huge market opportunity for businesses in this space.

2. **Favorable Policies and Regulations**: Governments and regulatory bodies worldwide are supporting the development and commercialization of lab-grown meat products. Motivated by environmental and public health factors, policymakers are actively creating regulatory frameworks that facilitate the transition to environmentally friendly protein sources.

3. **Technological Advancements**: In 2024, technological advancements in cell culture techniques, bioreactor engineering, and process scale-up have significantly reduced the cost of lab-grown meat production. The accessibility of these technologies provides a more feasible and affordable entry point for start-ups, facilitating the growth of the industry.

4. **Collaborative Opportunities**: A lab-grown meat start-up can leverage the symbiotic relationships that exist within the industry by collaborating with research institutions, technology providers, and other industry players, further improving product quality and reducing production costs.

Getting Started with a Lab-Grown Meat Production Start-Up:

1. **Develop a Unique Value Proposition**: Determine the product's key positioning and differentiation factors, such as focusing on a particular type of meat, developing unique textures and flavors, or specializing in a specific market segment.

2. **Market Research and Feasibility Analysis**: Conduct thorough market research and analysis to gauge consumer interest, identify potential competitors, and determine the appropriate pricing strategy for the target market. Calculate the required investments, profit margins, and projected break-even points to ensure feasibility.

3. **Establish a Research and Development Team**: Recruit a team of scientists, engineers, and food specialists to engage in research and development activities with the goal of optimizing production processes and improving the taste, texture, and composition of lab-grown meat products.

4. **Strategic Partnerships and Collaborations**: Forge partnerships with research institutions, technology providers, and other industry players to secure access to necessary resources and expertise. These partnerships can also provide support and guidance for navigating legal and regulatory requirements.

5. **Develop and Implement a Scaling Strategy**: Design an effective scaling strategy to transition from small-scale lab production to large-scale commercial production, ensuring the optimized utilization of resources and continued product quality improvements at larger scales.

6. **Regulatory Compliance**: Pay close attention to and comply with all applicable regulations and standards, both domestically and internationally. Establish a strong relationship with regulatory bodies to ensure smooth navigation through the product approval process.

7. **Marketing and Distribution**: Create a cohesive marketing strategy that effectively communicates the product's unique value proposition and addresses consumer concerns. Establish a robust distribution network to ensure efficient delivery of lab-grown meat products to end consumers.

By considering these factors and following the outlined steps, starting a lab-grown meat production business in 2024 has the potential to yield significant rewards as the world continues to embrace sustainable and ethical alternatives to traditional animal-based protein sources.

JAIME GEHLY

Minimalist Living and Lifestyle Consulting

In recent years, there has been a global paradigm shift towards minimalist living and lifestyle practices. This growing trend emphasizes simplicity, resourcefulness, and intentional living while minimizing clutter, excessive consumerism, and stress. In light of its increasing popularity, a minimalist living and lifestyle consulting start-up business presents a lucrative opportunity for 2024.

There are several reasons why this venture is a smart and successful choice:

1. **Growing Market Demand**: As people become more environmentally conscious and increasingly experience the effects of a fast-paced, consumer-driven society, they are seeking ways to simplify their lives, reduce their ecological footprint, and achieve balance. A consulting start-up that offers tools and guidance to help them transition towards a minimalist lifestyle will be in high demand.

2. **Positive Environmental Impact**: The adoption of minimalist practices contributes to decreasing waste and resource consumption, thereby reducing pressure on the environment. This factor will notably appeal to environmentally conscious individuals and organizations, providing a broad market for the start-up business.

3. **Wide-Ranging Services and Clientele**: The minimalist lifestyle is applicable to various aspects, such as home organization, personal finance, work-life balance, and wardrobe management. This range creates opportunities to cater to diverse client needs, from individuals looking to declutter their homes to businesses striving for sustainable practices.

4. **Flexibility and Scalability**: The start-up can be initiated with low overhead costs, catering to local clients, and later scale up to reach a broader or even international audience with online consultations, workshops, and digital resources.

5. **Substantial Benefits for Clients**: Adopting a minimalist lifestyle enables clients to reduce stress, improve mental well-being, save money, and cultivate healthier relationships with their surroundings. These transformative results will ensure a steady stream of clients seeking the start-up's services for guidance and support.

To Establish a Successful Minimalist Living and Lifestyle Consulting Start-Up, Follow These Basic Steps:

1. **Identify Your Niche and Services**: Determine which aspects of minimalist living you will specialize in and define the consulting services you will provide, such as workshops, one-on-one consultations, or online courses.

2. **Conduct Market Research**: Analyze your potential competitors and identify your target clientele, understanding their needs and preferences to ensure your offerings will resonate with them.

3. **Develop a Business Plan**: Outline your venture's objectives, strategies, expected costs, projected revenue, and growth plans. This comprehensive roadmap is crucial for attracting investment and guiding your future activities.

4. **Acquire Necessary Certifications and Licenses**: Based on your niche and local requirements, pursue relevant professional certifications and obtain any necessary licenses or permits to operate your consulting business legally.

5. **Create a Strong Online Presence**: Develop an engaging and informative website and maintain active social media accounts to showcase your expertise, services, and success stories, engaging potential clients and establishing credibility.

6. **Market Your Business**: Leverage various marketing channels, such as social media advertisements, content marketing, and local events, to raise awareness about your start-up and attract clients.

7. **Seek Collaborations and Networking Opportunities**: Connect with complementary businesses, local associations, and influencers to promote your services, pursue joint ventures, and expand your brand visibility.

By providing valuable guidance to individuals and organizations seeking a minimalist lifestyle, this start-up business will be well-positioned for success in the thriving contemporary culture of simplicity and sustainability.

Gamified E-Learning Apps

In the constantly evolving educational landscape, a gamified e-learning app start-up is primed for success in 2024. The global pandemic has accelerated the need for effective and engaging online learning solutions, with the demand for these platforms projected to increase rapidly in the coming years.

Why Gamified E-Learning Apps:

1. **A Rapidly Growing Market**: The global e-learning market is expected to reach $375 billion by 2026, with an increasing demand for online educational content.

2. **Appeals to Diverse Learners**: Gamified e-learning apps can effectively engage learners across subjects and age groups by adapting content to the user's unique preferences, prior knowledge, and learning pace.

3. **Improved Learning Outcomes**: Studies show that gamification enhances students' motivation, engagement, and academic performance, making the learning experience more enjoyable and productive.

4. **Lower Barriers to Entry**: With the widespread availability of smartphones and tablets, a gamified e-learning app has far-reaching potential to reach underserved populations with limited access to traditional education resources.

Basic Steps to Launch a Gamified E-Learning App Start-up:

1. **Define Your Niche**: Research the market to identify gaps and choose a specific target audience, such as school-aged students, adult learners, or professional development seekers.

2. **Develop a Business Plan**: Establish your company's mission, vision, goals, and key performance indicators (KPIs). Determine your start-up costs, a timeline for implementation, and a revenue model.

3. **Design Engaging Content and Interface**: The success of your app hinges on its ability to engage and entertain while simultaneously educating. Implement elements like storytelling, rewards, challenge scenarios, and feedback loops to create a captivating learning experience.

4. **Choose the Right Technology**: Select an appropriate technological infrastructure that meets your audience's preferences, along with a scalable framework to accommodate potential growth.

5. **Assemble a Skilled Team**: Recruit and hire knowledgeable individuals to handle roles like educational content creation, app development, marketing, and customer support.

6. **Ensure Privacy and Compliance**: Familiarize yourself with relevant data protection regulations (like GDPR) and establish protocols for safeguarding user data.

7. **Market Your App**: Develop a marketing strategy to raise awareness and generate interest. This may include search engine optimization (SEO), social media promotion, partnerships with educational institutions, or influencer endorsements.

A gamified e-learning app start-up in 2024 will experience significant growth, fueled by increased demand for accessible, engaging, and personalized educational content. By taking advantage of this trend and following the steps outlined above, entrepreneurs have the opportunity to create a smart and successful business venture that is poised to make a remarkable impact in the world of education.

Locavore Meal-Kit Delivery Services

In recent years, there has been a steadily growing interest in the concept of a "locavore" diet, emphasizing the consumption of locally produced food. This trend has picked up popularity due to the increasing awareness of the environmental, health, and economic benefits associated with local food systems. In 2024, starting a Locavore meal-kit delivery services business is not only timely, but it also presents a smart and lucrative opportunity. This business model combines convenience and health benefits while promoting support for local communities and environmental sustainability. The following summary presents the strong reasons behind this choice and outlines the steps necessary to start this business successfully.

Why it's a Smart Choice:

1. **Consumer Trends**: Consumers are progressively gravitating toward healthier, ethical, and environmentally friendly food production practices. This means that an increasing number of households are seeking services that provide a convenient way to eat locally sourced, fresh, and healthy meals. A Locavore meal-kit delivery service directly addresses this consumer demand and is thus better positioned for success.

2. **Environmental Sustainability**: Local food consumption helps reduce the carbon footprint associated with conventional food distribution, as it shortens the distance food travels from farm to table. Launching a Locavore meal-kit delivery service echoes the growing awareness of climate change and environmental issues in society, making it a prescient strategic choice.

3. **Economic Sustainability**: By sourcing ingredients and supplies from local farmers and producers, a Locavore meal-kit delivery business will contribute to local economic development. This not only ensures better quality control but also builds strong relationships with community partners.

101 BEST START-UP BUSINESS IDEAS FOR 2024 ACCORDING TO ADVANCED A.I.

Basic Steps to Get Started:

1. **Market Research**: Conduct thorough research to understand your target customers, their preferences, and dietary requirements. Investigate the competition to devise an effective business model and identify your unique selling points.

2. **Business Plan**: Develop a detailed business plan outlining your company's mission, target market, financial projections, and growth strategies. This document will be crucial in securing funding and partners for your start-up.

3. **Local Supplier Partnerships**: Establish connections with local farmers and producers to ensure a reliable supply of fresh, seasonal ingredients. Building strong relationships with these partners guarantees high-quality ingredients and allows for marketing collaboration and promotion.

4. **Menu Planning & Pricing**: Hire a skilled nutritionist and/or chef to design meal plans that cater to different dietary needs and preferences. Develop pricing strategies that account for production costs while remaining competitive in the market.

5. **Legal and Licensing**: Obtain necessary permits, licenses, and insurance for your business. Depending on local regulations, this may include food handling, public health, and zoning permits.

6. **Online Platform Development**: Create a user-friendly website and mobile application for your meal-kit delivery service. This platform should be easy to navigate and have robust security features to protect customer information.

7. **Marketing & Branding**: Develop a strong brand identity that highlights the locavore and environmental values of your business. Use social media, email campaigns, and word-of-mouth to generate buzz and attract customers to your service.

Starting a Locavore meal-kit delivery service in 2024 is a smart choice given the growing consumer interest in healthier, locally sourced foods and an increased awareness of environmental sustainability. By following these basic steps and building a strong business plan, this start-up idea can harness the potential to create a successful and environmentally responsible brand.

JAIME GEHLY

Hyper-Local News Apps

In the digital age with rapidly evolving technology and an increasing need for relevant, trustworthy news, starting a hyper-local news app business in 2024 offers a significant opportunity to fill a gap in the news industry. By focusing on local, community-driven news, this start-up model has the potential to be both smart and successful. To achieve this, understanding your target audience, partnering with local advertisers, leveraging artificial intelligence and machine learning technologies, and selecting the right team and collaborators will be key steps in setting the foundation for this venture.

Key Factors to Success:

1. **Identifying the Market Gap**: Traditional news media often overlook local stories and issues, focusing instead on national or international news. A hyper-local news app that curates and delivers news to a specific neighborhood or small community addresses this void by connecting users with nearby stories and events that are relevant to them. Moreover, as people are becoming increasingly concerned with fake news, trust in local sources has risen, giving credibility to localized news apps.

2. **Expanding Advertising Opportunities**: A hyper-local news app provides ample opportunities to partner with local businesses and organizations for highly targeted advertisement placements. The app's specific, localized focus appeals to advertisers who can efficiently reach their target customers based on geographic location, increasing user engagement and the likelihood of the business succeeding.

3. **Embracing New Technologies**: By leveraging artificial intelligence (AI) and machine learning algorithms, the hyper-local news app can serve personalized, high-quality content to users based on their preferences and behavior in real-time. AI-powered content aggregation and analysis ensures that the app offers accurate and timely news, further strengthening user trust and retention.

4. **Building the Right Team**: To create a successful hyper-local news app, a team with diverse skills is necessary – including developers, designers, data analysts, journalists, and marketers. Combining local journalism talent with expertise in new technologies will propel the start-up toward success by ensuring relevant, reliable, and high-quality news that resonates with its audience.

5. **Identifying Collaborators and Partnerships**: Developing partnerships with trusted local media outlets or independent contributors can enrich the app's content offerings, creating a diverse range of perspectives and valuable information. These partnerships also help establish credibility, resources, and support during the initial start-up phase.

6. **Launching a User-Centric App**: Designing an intuitive and user-friendly app is vital for efficient user engagement and retention. To achieve this, invest in a market study and user testing to understand the audience's needs and expectations while refining and iterating the app's design and features.

7. **Preparing for Monetization**: To create a sustainable business model, plan for a mix of revenue streams – such as subscription plans, sponsored content, and advertising partnerships. Determine the right balance between revenue generation and user experience to ensure both long-term financial stability and user satisfaction.

In conclusion, starting a hyper-local news app business in 2024 is a smart and promising undertaking with the potential to succeed in the digital age. By addressing the market gap, embracing new technologies, and focusing on user-centric experiences, this start-up model can effectively disrupt and innovate within the evolving news industry.

JAIME GEHLY

Electric Vehicle Charging Stations

In 2024, the accelerating transition to electric vehicles (EVs) presents an exceptional opportunity for businesses to capitalize on the growing demand for efficient and accessible charging infrastructure. Starting an EV charging station business can offer numerous benefits, including sustainable profits, attractive incentives, and the prospect of contributing to a greener future.

Market Growth and Demand: The automobile industry is witnessing a significant shift in consumer preferences towards electric vehicles as a result of increased environmental awareness, strict emissions regulations, and advancements in battery technology. Major automakers are projected to increase EV production in the coming years, effectively expanding the target market for charging infrastructure. By establishing a network of electric vehicle charging stations, start-ups can effectively cater to this increasing demand.

Government Support and Incentives: Governments around the world are pushing for rapid EV adoption by providing various incentives and support for charging station infrastructure, making it a favorable investment. These incentives may include subsidies, reduced taxes, and rebates, all of which contribute to bridging the gap between the traditional fueling infrastructure and the emerging EV charging landscape.

High ROI and Revenue Streams: Investing in an electric vehicle charging station start-up offers a high return on investment (ROI) due to the relatively low operational and maintenance costs compared to traditional fueling stations. Additionally, businesses can diversify their revenue streams by offering value-added services, such as charging subscriptions, advertising, and retail opportunities within the charging stations.

Steps to Get Started:

1. **Market Research**: Conduct comprehensive market research to understand current and future EV trends, customer needs, and competitor analysis. This will help identify the demands and facilitate informed decision-making throughout the start-up process.

2. **Business Plan**: Develop a detailed business plan outlining your target audience, scope and objectives, product/services offering, financial projections, and marketing strategies.

3. **Location Analysis**: Site selection is crucial to the success of an EV charging station business. Choose strategic locations with high traffic, visibility, and convenient access to facilitate usage, such as near shopping centers, highway rest stops, or in dense urban areas.

4. **Legal Requirements**: Research and fulfill all legal requirements, obtain necessary permits, and comply with local and federal regulations for operating charging stations.

5. **Funding and Financial Support**: Identify potential sources of funding and incentives to finance your start-up. This may include government incentives, grants, loans, or seeking investors and partners.

6. **Procurement and Installation**: Partner with reliable and reputable EV charging equipment manufacturers to procure and install the necessary charging infrastructure. Consider offering a mix of charging speeds and compatibility with various EV models.

7. **Marketing and Brand Awareness**: Implement marketing strategies to build brand awareness and promote your charging stations to potential users. This may include targeted advertising, social media presence, and partnerships with local businesses or EV manufacturers.

8. **Maintenance and Customer Support**: Establish a team to oversee maintenance for the charging stations and offer exceptional customer service to ensure a positive user experience.

An electric vehicle charging station start-up in 2024 presents a lucrative and future-oriented business opportunity, as the global transition to electric vehicles accelerates. By performing thorough market research and following a meticulous start-up plan, business owners can tap into this rapidly growing market, ensuring long-term success and contributing to a greener future.

Smart Eldercare Solutions

By 2024, the demand for eldercare solutions is expected to rise significantly as a consequence of an increased aging population and the rapid growth of technology. A smart eldercare solutions start-up can capitalize on these market dynamics to develop a successful business providing essential services for aging individuals and their families. Offering innovative eldercare solutions through a start-up business model allows for better adaptation to the continually changing technological and social landscape.

Market Analysis:

In recent years, there has been a global surge in the number of seniors, with estimates suggesting that by 2050, there will be over two billion people aged 60 and above. This trend is creating a challenge for traditional eldercare solutions which are unable to handle the volume and unique needs of the elderly population. Subsequently, it has led to the emergence of smart eldercare solutions - an integration of innovative technologies and advanced services. It is here that a start-up finds its opportunity to deliver efficient solutions, offering smart services that cater to elderly individuals at home, in care facilities, and beyond.

Competitive Landscape:

As the market for eldercare solutions expands, so does the competition. While established businesses primarily rely on traditional care systems, start-ups have a unique opportunity to disrupt the industry with smart technology, robotic solutions, and advanced remote care services. By identifying gaps in the market and leveraging innovative technologies, a start-up can position itself as a prominent solution provider in the eldercare industry.

Basic Steps to Get Started:

1. **Market Research & Gap Analysis**: Conduct comprehensive market research to identify potential gaps and niches in the eldercare market that can be addressed by smart technology and digital solutions.

2. **Business Plan**: Develop a detailed business plan outlining the start-up's objectives, target audience, proposed products or services, revenue models, and marketing strategies.

3. **Gather a Skilled Team**: Build a team with a diverse set of skills, including experts in eldercare, technology, design, and business development, to ensure the development of efficient and technologically advanced solutions.

4. **Identify Technology & Partnership Opportunities**: Explore alliances with other leading companies or start-ups in the healthcare, technology, or AI sectors to boost credibility and enhance technological capabilities.

5. **Legal & Compliance**: Ensure compliance with local and international eldercare and healthcare regulations. Consult with legal experts to develop appropriate contracts, policies, and protect intellectual property rights.

6. **Funding**: Secure funding through venture capitalists, angel investors, or government grants to initiate product development, marketing, and initial operational setup.

7. **Product & Service Development**: Create user-focused, accessible, and innovative products and services using the latest technology trends such as the Internet of Things (IoT), machine learning, and AI.

8. **Marketing Strategy**: Design and execute a marketing plan that targets senior care providers, families, and elderly individuals themselves to create awareness about the start-up's smart eldercare solutions.

9. **Continuous Improvement**: Regularly update and upgrade products and services based on user feedback and market needs, and monitor competitors to anticipate and respond to industry changes quickly.

In 2024, a smart eldercare solutions start-up has the potential to revolutionize the eldercare industry by offering technologically advanced solutions designed to meet the rising demand for elderly care services. By embracing market opportunities and following the outlined steps, the start-up can achieve significant success and contribute positively to the well-being of seniors around the world.

On-Demand House Cleaning Services

The demand for house cleaning services is projected to grow steadily in 2024, driven by factors such as increasing urbanization, a growing middle class, and the gig economy. Starting an on-demand house cleaning services business is a smart and successful choice for aspiring entrepreneurs seeking a scalable, flexible, and profitable venture. This brief summary will explore the reasons behind this success and outline the essential steps needed to launch a successful start-up.

1. **Growing Market Demand**: The fast-paced lives of urban dwellers and a rising number of dual-income households have led to an increasing demand for time-saving solutions like house cleaning services. In 2024, more people will value their time and seek convenient, on-demand services to maintain a clean and healthy living environment. Leveraging this trend can position a business to capitalize on the expanding market opportunities.

2. **Scalable Business Model**: On-demand house cleaning services offer a highly scalable model, enabling the business to grow as demand increases. By using a digital platform to connect service providers with customers, the start-up can cut staffing costs and avoid the expense of setting up brick-and-mortar facilities, allowing the company to expand with a lean structure.

3. **Flexibility & Convenience**: As an intrinsic part of the gig economy, on-demand house cleaning provides flexible job opportunities for both service providers and consumers. For cleaners, the business offers the ability to work on their terms, while consumers benefit from the convenience of having instant access to professional, trusted cleaning services.

Steps to Launch an On-demand House Cleaning Start-up:

Identify the Target Market: Determine the specific demographic and geographic areas you intend to serve. This includes conducting market research and competitor analysis to ensure gaps and opportunities exist in the market.

Develop a Business Plan: Establish your business strategy, including your unique selling proposition, pricing, revenue model, and marketing plans. Establish a budget and financial projections to guide your venture.

Register Your Business: Choose a suitable name for the start-up and register your business according to local laws and regulations. Ensure you have the necessary business licenses and permits in place.

Build a Digital Platform: Create a user-friendly and secure online web or mobile platform that efficiently connects service providers with customers. Ensure the platform features an intuitive booking system, secure payment gateway, and rating/feedback system.

Curate a Reliable Cleaning Service Provider Network: Rigorously vet potential cleaning service providers for their qualifications, experience, and background to guarantee high-quality service to customers.

Implement Insurance and Liability Protections: Secure insurance coverage for the business, the cleaning professionals, and your clients' properties to minimize risks.

Develop a Marketing Plan: Design a marketing mix – digital and offline – that will target your ideal customers, create brand awareness, and generate a steady flow of bookings.

Manage Operations and Customer Experience: Implement best practices and efficient communication channels to ensure smooth operations, customer satisfaction, and high-quality service delivery.

In conclusion, an on-demand house cleaning services start-up in 2024 is a promising venture with enormous growth potential. By focusing on meeting customer needs, offering flexibility and convenience, and carefully curating service providers, the business can achieve remarkable success in the rapidly evolving marketplace.

JAIME GEHLY

Coworking Space Management Solutions

The burgeoning gig economy, increased remote work culture, and the emphasis on cost-effective and flexible solutions to traditional office spaces have paved the way for coworking space businesses. Establishing a coworking space management solutions start-up in 2024 stands to be a smart and successful choice, capitalizing on the evolving work dynamics and addressing the needs of the growing coworking space market. To establish a thriving business in this sector, entrepreneurs must follow a series of basic steps – from conducting market research and analyzing trends, to implementing sustainable solutions, and focusing on excellent customer service.

Market Research and Analysis: Understanding the current and future coworking landscape is essential for developing tailored business strategies. Analyzing market trends, potential customer segments, and competitors can help determine the most attractive business niches and target markets, such as scalability for small businesses, high-end coworking spaces for bigger companies, or specialized spaces for specific industries. Like any other start-up, a coworking space management solutions business must leverage existing and emerging technologies that increase efficiency, convenience, and security.

Securing Investments and Developing a Business Plan: Coworking space start-ups must secure financial investment, either through self-funding, loans, or attracting investors. A well-structured and comprehensive business plan addressing financial projections, marketing strategies, risk management, and sustainability measures is crucial to attracting investors and securing the necessary funds.

Finding the Ideal Location: The key to a successful coworking space management solutions start-up is finding the right location that suits the target audience and is easily accessible. Entrepreneurs must consider factors like nearby transportation options, local amenities, and the surrounding business ecosystem to better meet the needs of their customers and enhance the overall coworking experience.

Designing and Equipping the Workspace: The interior design and layout of a coworking space play a vital role in attracting customers and ensuring their productivity. Spaces should be optimized to encourage collaboration, creativity, and flexibility, while also offering private areas for focused work. Equipping the space with the latest technology, ensuring ergonomic furniture options, and ample access to resources like high-speed internet, phone booths, and meeting rooms promote a more wholesome coworking experience.

Implementing Sustainable Solutions: As environmental concerns become more prominent, businesses that adopt and promote sustainable practices tend to be more attractive. A coworking space management solutions start-up can stand out by incorporating green technology, energy efficiency measures, and waste management systems, consequently attracting environmentally conscious clientele.

Focusing on Customer Service and Community Building: To successfully retain customers, coworking space start-ups should aim to cultivate a positive user experience, offer tailored services and plans, and regularly solicit client feedback to adapt and improve. Establishing a coworking community where businesses and entrepreneurs can collaborate, network, and support one another can help boost overall appeal and brand image.

Marketing and Promotion: A successful start-up takes advantage of traditional, digital, and social media channels to create awareness and drive customer engagement. To build a prominent online presence, invest in content marketing, social media campaigns, and SEO optimization. Offline marketing strategies, including hosting events, workshops, and partnering with local businesses, can help bring valuable footfall to the coworking space.

In conclusion, starting a coworking space management solutions business in 2024 is a smart choice considering the changing work landscape and market demand. By following these basic steps and focusing on user experience, a start-up in this sector can thrive in the coming years, offering both flexibility and productivity to customers.

JAIME GEHLY

Virtual Coworking Spaces

Virtual coworking spaces are anticipated to be a highly successful and profitable business venture for small start-ups in 2024. The prominence of remote work, cost savings for businesses, demand for flexible work environments, and advancements in technology contribute to this success. To start a virtual coworking space, entrepreneurs should plan their niche, create a robust digital infrastructure, develop effective communication channels, offer value-added services and support, and implement a strong marketing strategy.

The unprecedented rise in remote work in recent years has created a surge in demand for virtual coworking spaces. Small businesses and start-ups can capitalize on this opportunity in 2024, as these spaces offer several benefits that improve both the likelihood of success and the profitability of the venture.

1. **Remote Work Trend**: Remote work has become ubiquitous due to digital transformation, which led companies to adapt quickly to a distributed workforce. This change in work culture makes virtual coworking spaces an ideal choice for the future where the workforce is increasingly decentralized.

2. **Cost Savings**: Virtual coworking spaces help businesses save on overhead expenses associated with traditional office spaces. Small businesses can benefit from reduced expenses by investing in a virtual coworking space, which allows them to allocate their resources more efficiently.

3. **Demand for Flexibility**: The demand for flexible work environments continues to grow, as workers increasingly value the ability to work from any location. Virtual coworking spaces provide this freedom and flexibility, making them an appealing option for both clients and businesses.

4. **Technological Advancements**: Recent advancements in technology, such as virtual reality and artificial intelligence, have made the development and management of virtual coworking spaces more seamless and efficient. These technological innovations have opened up new opportunities for start-ups targeting this market.

Starting a Virtual Coworking Space Business Requires Careful Planning and Strategic Execution. Here Are the Basic Steps One Needs to Take:

1. **Plan Your Niche**: Determine the target market for your virtual coworking space. It may cater to specific industries or focus on offering tailored experiences for different business types.

2. **Create a Digital Infrastructure**: Invest in developing a user-friendly, secure virtual platform that provides a seamless experience for clients while offering necessary digital resources such as video conferencing, project management tools, and cloud storage.

3. **Develop Communication Channels**: Implement efficient communication tools that enable members to collaborate effectively while maintaining a sense of community.

4. **Offer Value-Added Services and Support**: In addition to providing a coworking space, offer services such as mentorship, business support, networking opportunities, workshops, and resources to attract and retain clients.

5. **Marketing Strategy**: Plan and execute a robust marketing strategy, leveraging multiple channels such as social media, content marketing, and targeted advertisements to attract potential clients to your virtual coworking space.

In conclusion, the growing trend of remote work and technological advancements indicate that a virtual coworking space start-up is well poised for success in 2024. By identifying the target niche, creating a strong digital infrastructure, and offering value-added services, small businesses can capitalize on this profitable opportunity in the coworking industry.

JAIME GEHLY

Content Personalization Services

Content personalization has become a critical aspect of modern marketing strategies, making it a promising opportunity for start-ups. A content personalization service start-up is poised to witness tremendous growth and success in 2024. This one-page summary highlights why content personalization services are essential and outlines the initial steps required to launch a start-up in this domain.

Key Factors:

1. **Increased Demand for Personalized Content**: As the digital landscape continues to expand, customers are being bombarded by information. In 2024, personalization will be more critical than ever. Businesses will require content personalization services to curate and deliver tailor-made experiences to their audience. This growing need presents an ideal opportunity for a start-up to step in, capitalize on the demand, and create a thriving business.

2. **Improved User Experience and Customer Satisfaction**: Personalized content creates a better user experience by providing more relevant and engaging content. A content personalization start-up will help businesses tailor their content to suit individual customer's preferences, improving customer satisfaction rates and nurturing long-term relationships.

3. **Increased Engagement and Conversion Rates**: By providing personalized content to users, businesses will witness higher engagement and improved conversion rates. As a result, investing in a content personalization service start-up is a lucrative prospect with potential for high returns.

4. **Emergence of AI & Big Data**: The rise of AI technologies and big data analytics enables content personalization services to be more effective than ever before. These advancements allow start-ups to create personalized experiences for users in real-time, further augmenting the value proposition of content personalization.

To Start a Content Personalization Service Business in 2024, the Following Basic Steps are Recommended:

1. **Market Research**: Conduct thorough market research to understand the current market landscape and target audience. Identify gaps in the market, potential competitors, and target segments.

2. **Defining Your Value Proposition**: Develop a unique value proposition that differentiates your start-up from competitors. Showcase how your services will provide unparalleled personalized experiences to its users.

3. **Business Plan & Model**: Create a detailed business plan, including your objectives, products, customer segments, revenue streams, and resources required. Determine the most suitable business model (B2B, B2C, or B2B2C) based on your target market and services.

4. **Building the Team**: Assemble a team with diverse skill sets spanning content creation, AI and data analytics, marketing, and IT support. Your team should possess a strong understanding of content personalization and a passion for delivering exceptional user experiences.

5. **Develop the Platform and Services**: Leverage AI and big data technologies to build a scalable content personalization platform that allows businesses to create targeted campaigns and personalized content experiences for their users.

6. **Legal and Regulatory Requirements**: Ensure compliance with all legal and regulatory requirements. Obtain necessary licenses, patents, or trademarks. Set up contractual agreements and partnerships, if required.

7. **Marketing and Sales Strategy**: Create a robust marketing and sales plan, covering aspects such as branding, targeting, promotion, and advertising. Utilize both traditional and digital channels to generate traction and awareness for your content personalization service start-up.

In conclusion, a content personalization service start-up in 2024 is an excellent business opportunity with high growth potential. By positioning itself at the forefront of personalized content, the start-up will cater to evolving market needs, leveraging new technologies and delivering value-added services that significantly impact business performances.

Micro-Investing/Stocks Trading Platforms

The growing interest in investment and financial markets, along with the rapid development of technology, makes starting a micro-investing and stocks trading platform an excellent business opportunity in 2024. This sector has experienced strong growth and high levels of innovation in recent years, offering easy-to-use and accessible solutions to a wide range of users. By leveraging advanced technology, targeting an untapped audience, and delivering value-added services, a start-up in this field can greatly benefit from the expanding market.

Key Factors for Success in 2024:

1. **Widespread Adoption of Smartphone Technology**: With the majority of the population owning smartphones, micro-investing platforms can now reach a broader and previously untapped audience. The ubiquity of smartphones allows start-ups to create user-friendly apps that make investing accessible and engaging for novice users, thereby driving growth in this market.

2. **Growing Interest in Investment**: An increasing number of individuals are looking to invest and grow their financial assets. This presents a great opportunity for micro-investment platforms, as they can offer an entry point to the stock market for people who are new to investing or who may not have large amounts of capital.

3. **Financial Inclusion**: Micro-investing platforms provide an opportunity for financial inclusion, enabling users who are underrepresented or underserved in traditional financial markets to begin building wealth. This will be essential in expanding the user base and ensuring the long-term success of the platform.

4. **Advanced Technology and Automation**: The opportunities offered by artificial intelligence and machine learning can be leveraged to create personalized investment recommendations based on individual preferences, risk tolerance, and financial goals. The use of such technology will also allow for cost-effective, automated portfolio management, which will be key in attracting and retaining users.

Basic Steps to Get Started:

1. **Market Research**: Conduct thorough research on the target audience, competition, trends, and regulations in the financial industry. This will help identify market gaps and opportunities, as well as determine the platform's unique selling point.

2. **Develop a Business Model**: Establish the financial structure, services, and revenue streams of the platform. Consider offering tiered subscription plans, charging fees for premium features, or generating income through affiliate marketing and referrals.

3. **Platform Development**: Create a user-friendly and intuitive app or web platform that incorporates advanced technology, security features, and seamless integration with external financial systems. Ensure that the platform complies with regulatory requirements and industry standards.

4. **Assemble an Expert Team**: Recruit a team of professionals with expertise in finance, technology, marketing, and customer support to manage and drive the growth of the start-up. This will ensure that the platform provides a comprehensive and reliable service.

5. **Marketing and Customer Acquisition**: Implement a robust marketing strategy that targets the identified user segments through various digital channels, including social media, online advertising, and content marketing. Collaborate with influencers, bloggers, and media outlets to generate buzz and credibility around the platform.

6. **Continuous Improvement and Expansion**: Evaluate platform performance regularly through client feedback, market analysis, and industry benchmarks. Adapt and improve the platform in response to changing market conditions and user preferences. Furthermore, explore expansion strategies, such as entering new markets or offering additional financial services.

In conclusion, a micro-investing/stocks trading platform start-up presents a promising business opportunity in 2024. By leveraging technology, ensuring financial inclusion, and catering to an expanding user base, ambitious entrepreneurs can create a successful and sustainable business in this rapidly evolving industry.

JAIME GEHLY

Home-Schooling Tools and Resources

In recent years, there has been an increasing desire for personalized education options as well as a growth in remote learning environments. By 2024, a home-schooling tools and resources start-up business is in an advantageous position to capitalize on this trend, offering a wide range of customized curricula, educational resources, and learning tools tailored to each child's unique needs. This summary will outline why home-schooling is a promising business sector and cover the basic steps required to launch a successful start-up in this industry.

Market Opportunity:

1. **Demand Growth**: As a consequence of the pandemic, remote and online learning methods have been adopted worldwide. These methods are likely to continue to grow in popularity, expanding the home-schooling market.

2. **Technology Integration**: Advancements in technology and widespread accessibility of the internet provide better opportunities for home-based learning solutions. A start-up focusing on these tools and resources can help families create technology-driven, engaging learning experiences.

3. **Personalization**: Parents are increasingly seeking a more personalized education for their children that can cater to individual learning styles and preferences. A home-schooling tools and resources start-up can swiftly adapt and meet this demand by offering customization in the learning process.

Basic Steps to Start a Home-Schooling Tools and Resources Start-Up:

1. **Market Research**: Conduct in-depth research to identify the target audience's needs and preferences, and to assess the competition, trends, and market opportunities. This will guide the focus of the start-up and its service offerings.

2. **Business Plan**: Create a comprehensive business plan that covers objectives, target market, product offerings, pricing models, market analysis, competition, marketing strategies, and financial projections.

3. **Legal Aspects**: Choose a suitable business structure, consult with an attorney to understand necessary legal requirements, and register the business. Also, seek any necessary permits or licenses to operate the start-up.

4. **Develop Products and Services**: Design and create tailored curricula, educational resources, and tools, integrating innovative learning methods and technology. Focus on high-quality, engaging content that meets the diverse needs of home-schooling families.

5. **Partnerships**: Collaborate with subject matter experts, experienced educators, and education technology providers to develop a varied product offering and support system for users.

6. **Marketing and Advertising**: Implement a robust digital marketing strategy utilizing social media, content marketing, SEO, and targeted advertising to reach prospective clients. Leverage testimonials, success stories, and showcasing features of the start-up's offerings to generate organic growth.

7. **Funding**: Seek funding through potential sources such as angel investors, venture capitalists, crowdfunding platforms or small-business loans, depending on the financial needs and requirements of the start-up.

8. **Customer Support and Feedback**: Develop a strong customer support system and regularly gather feedback from users to continuously improve products, services, and user experience.

A home-schooling tools and resources start-up business in 2024 represents a compelling investment opportunity, granting families access to personalized educational experiences and making use of evolving technology. By taking a systematic approach, entrepreneurs can build a successful business that effectively meets the demands of the growing home-schooling market while fostering a culture of innovative learning.

AI-Driven Content Marketing Tools

The potential of AI-driven content marketing tools has been realized in recent years, with a range of benefits such as accelerated content creation, increased audience engagement, and improved decision making. Due to the rapid advancement of AI and machine learning technologies, the demand for AI-driven content marketing tools is set to surge in the coming years, making it a lucrative business opportunity for startups.

Market Potential:

1. **Higher Demand for Content Marketing**: With an increasing number of companies realizing that content marketing is a cost-effective way to drive customer engagement and create brand awareness, the demand for AI-driven content marketing solutions is expected to grow exponentially by 2024.

2. **Scalability**: AI-powered content marketing tools provide scalability to businesses, allowing them to handle larger amounts of content and more complex marketing campaigns, thus driving increased demand for these services.

3. **Personalization**: As consumers demand highly personalized and engaging content, AI-driven content marketing tools can analyze data and create tailored content for niche audiences, offering unique opportunities for startups to cater to these specific customer preferences.

4. **Improved ROI**: AI-driven content marketing solutions provide businesses with more accurate insights through data analytics and predictive algorithms, enabling the creation of highly effective and targeted campaigns maximizing ROI.

Steps to Get Started:

1. **Market Research**: Conduct thorough research into the target market including competitor analysis, audience profiles, and the latest AI-driven content marketing technologies.

2. **Business Plan**: Develop a comprehensive business plan outlining the startup's goals, target market, competitive advantages, revenue models, marketing strategies, and financial projections.

3. **Technical Development**: Identify and acquire necessary technical expertise, whether through hiring skilled team members or partnering with organizations specializing in AI and machine learning.

4. **AI-Driven Content Marketing Tool Development**: Focus on creating innovative solutions that differentiate the startup's offerings from existing competitors, addressing key pain points and market gaps in content marketing.

5. **Funding**: Explore funding options, such as venture capital, angel investors, or government grants, to secure the financial resources required for the initial setup and operational costs.

6. **Legal and Compliance**: Ensure the startup complies with necessary regulations and has proper legal and intellectual property protections in place.

7. **Launch Strategy**: Develop a well thought out product launch plan, incorporating numerous marketing channels, including social media, search engine optimization (SEO), email marketing, public relations, and content marketing.

8. **Networking and Partnerships**: Establish connections with key industry players, influencers, and potential customers to build trust, credibility, and brand visibility in the market.

9. **Product Improvement and Expansion**: Continuously enhance and expand the product offering based on market feedback and user analysis to create a more robust and competitive solution.

With increasing demand for effective and personalized content marketing strategies, an AI-driven content marketing tools start-up business holds significant potential in 2024. By identifying key market gaps and tailoring the offering to cater to diverse customer needs, startups can drive technological progress and gain a competitive advantage in this emerging market. Ensuring a focused and comprehensive approach to product development, promotion, and continuous improvement remains crucial for long-term success.

Location and Activity-Based Social Networks

A location and activity-based social network start-up has the potential to become a highly profitable and influential business in 2024. Advances in technology, increased focus on active lifestyles, and the need for community-building are propelling growth in this market, making it an exciting opportunity for entrepreneurs. To get started with such a venture, founders must consider factors such as scalability, user privacy and satisfaction, and a monetization strategy.

Key Factors:

1. **Market Opportunity and Growth Drivers**: With the increasing adoption of smartphones, GPS technology, and rapid digital interconnectedness, it's no surprise that location-based services are gaining popularity. Additionally, the active lifestyle movement and a growing focus on mental and physical wellbeing are fueling the demand for niche social platforms. These platforms encourage individuals to explore and engage with activities and interests that align with their hobbies and lifestyle. Plus, community-driven connections foster new relationships and enrich users' personal and social lives.

2. **Unmet Needs and Competitive Advantage**: While various social networks currently exist, there remains a gap for a unified platform that specifically addresses activity-based socialization and location-driven experiences. A start-up providing a seamless, user-friendly platform that caters to the specific desires of its user base can gain a competitive edge over generalized social networks. By combining the best of both location-aware services and activity-based socializing, this start-up will create a unique niche in the market.

Key Steps in Starting an Activity-Based Social Network Start-Up:

1. **Conduct Market Research**: Identify the target audience and understand their needs, preferences, and behavior. Determine the primary features and functionalities that users seek from location and activity-based networks.

2. **Develop a Unique Value Proposition**: Articulate how your start-up will differentiate itself from competitors by addressing specific user needs, catering to untapped niches, and offering a superior user experience.

3. **Seek Legal and Regulatory Compliance**: Ensure you adhere to all relevant laws and regulations, particularly those related to privacy and data usage, as users value the protection of their personal information.

4. **Design and Develop the Platform**: Invest in a user-friendly interface that provides intuitive navigation and enticing visuals, while keeping content relevant and engaging. Utilize cutting-edge technologies, such as machine learning algorithms, to better understand user behavior and preferences.

5. **Test and Iterate**: Build a Minimum Viable Product (MVP) to test with a small group of users. Gather feedback and make enhancements as necessary before expanding to a larger audience.

6. **Marketing and User Acquisition**: Develop a comprehensive marketing strategy to build awareness and drive user adoption, utilizing social media, digital advertising, blog partnerships, and influencer endorsements.

7. **Monetization Strategy**: Determine the most suitable revenue model, such as in-app purchases, freemium offerings, or leveraging partnerships for sponsored content and events.

By addressing the growing demand for activity-focused social experiences, a location and activity-based social network start-up can capitalize on emerging trends and create immense value for users. A well-designed platform that fosters strong, genuine connections and prioritizes user satisfaction can differentiate itself in the market as a game-changer in 2024. The key to success will lie in understanding the target audience, offering tailored connections, and ensuring a robust, secure platform for users to explore and engage in their passions.

JAIME GEHLY

Personalized Learning AI for Kids

In the ever-evolving educational landscape of 2024, the importance of personalized learning experiences becomes increasingly evident. A start-up focusing on personalized learning AI for kids meets the growing needs of modern education, catering to the individual learning styles, pace, and abilities of each child. This shift to a more targeted and engaging education system is further supported by rapid technological advancements and increasing public interest. Below we outline a high-level overview of reasons why such start-ups show promising prospects and describe the steps involved in getting started.

Key Factors:

1. **Emergence of Personalized Learning**: The one-size-fits-all approach to education has proven inadequate in accommodating diverse learning needs. A personalized learning AI for kids provides an enriched learning experience by adapting to each child's individual strengths and challenges, delivering optimal instruction, guidance, and support. As education becomes increasingly important for growth in contemporary society, the demand for educational tools centered on tailored learning experiences is expected to be on the rise.

2. **Technology-Driven Education Transformation**: The improved processing power of devices, advanced data analytics, and integration of machine learning capabilities have paved the way for more intelligent and refined educational Environments. A personalized learning AI can leverage these advancements to deliver unique, intuitive, and dynamic learning content that adapts to the needs of each child.

3. **Scalability and Cost-Effectiveness**: AI-powered personalized learning platforms have the potential to scale education and make it more accessible. They can lower costs for individual users while consistently providing a high level of educational prowess. Start-ups in this field can tap into local, national, and international markets, benefiting from a wide range of potential customers.

4. **Parental and Institutional Investment**: Parents and education institutions alike have shown a growing interest in personalized learning opportunities, acknowledging their ability to pave the way for individual student success. This support can act as a foundation to propel start-ups to achieve mainstream appeal, driving both private and public investment into these initiatives.

Basic Steps Required to Get Started:

1. **Ideation and Research**: Conduct thorough market research to identify gaps in the education sector where personalized learning AI solutions can be impactful. Develop a foundational idea, mission, and vision for your start-up.

2. **Building a Team**: Assemble a team of interdisciplinary experts with experience in areas such as AI, machine learning, education, and business development. This will ensure well-rounded knowledge and effective decision making within the organization.

3. **Developing a Prototype**: Create a proof-of-concept model for your personalized learning AI program. This should include core functionalities, backend infrastructure, and user interface designs. Consider employing agile development methodologies to remain adaptable.

4. **Testing and Iterations**: Extensively test the developed prototype with target users, gathering feedback for improvements to the personalized learning AI. Make necessary revisions to enhance the efficiency and effectiveness of the system.

5. **Securing Funding**: Seek out investor partnerships, government grants, or crowdfunding opportunities to provide ample financial resources for development, marketing, and scaling of the start-up.

6. **Launch and Marketing**: Strategize and execute product launch campaigns, targeting potential customers and partners within the education sector. Utilize social media, public relations, content marketing, and other tactics to boost brand awareness and expand reach.

7. **Continuous Improvement**: Keep track of industry trends, technological advancements, and user feedback to continually improve the personalized learning AI, ensuring it remains relevant and beneficial.

In conclusion, a start-up focused on personalized learning AI for kids stands to make a tangible impact in the education sector of 2024, offering dynamic learning experiences tailored to each child's unique needs. With the proper planning and execution, this type of business can both thrive and contribute to a transformative shift in the way children learn.

JAIME GEHLY

Disaster Management and Risk Prediction Tools

A disaster management and risk prediction start-up would be highly successful in 2024 due to the increasing global vulnerability to natural disasters and climate change, amplified by urbanization, deforestation, and inefficient infrastructures. This start-up would create innovative solutions to help communities and governments make informed decisions, mitigate risks, and allocate resources effectively. The potential market for such a business is substantial, with increasing demand for solutions to manage and predict natural disasters.

Market Need and Potential: The frequency of natural disasters, such as floods, earthquakes, hurricanes, and wildfires, has been on a steady rise worldwide, putting immense stress on governments, businesses, and individuals. As climate change exacerbates these events, nations strive to strengthen their preventive and counteractive measures. The disaster management and risk prediction industry is receiving more and more attention, not only from governments but from private corporations and social organizations as well. These decision-makers will seek tailored tools that can analyze, predict, and manage disaster risks, generating a greater demand for such services.

Key Success Factors and Steps to Get Started:

1. **Validate the Business Idea**: Before proceeding, conduct a thorough market analysis and identify the specific needs of your target audience. This analysis should focus on understanding the potential customers, competition, and overall climate of the disaster management sector.

2. **Develop a Robust and Innovative Product**: Design a user-friendly, comprehensive, and adaptable disaster management software tool or system that can gather data from multiple sources, analyze risks, and provide accurate predictions. Incorporate emerging technologies such as Artificial Intelligence (AI), Machine Learning, and Big Data to enhance accuracy and broaden the scope of the tools/services offered.

3. **Build a Strong Founding Team with Diverse Skills**: Assemble a team of experts with different backgrounds including data science, disaster management, software development, and business development to ensure a well-rounded

strategy for success. This diverse team will help in making informed decisions and circumventing potential roadblocks.

4. **Seek Funding and Resources**: Secure adequate funding through avenues such as venture capital, government grants, or support from industry partners. This funding will be vital towards developing a strong and effective product and promoting growth.

5. **Establish Strategic Partnerships**: Collaborate with governments, non-governmental organizations (NGOs), aid agencies, insurance companies, and other stakeholders that require disaster management solutions. These partnerships will help in gaining valuable insights, expanding the start-up's network, and generating real-world use cases for validation and development.

6. **Develop a Solid Marketing Strategy**: Prioritize public relations, networking, and online visibility. Clearly communicate the unique selling points and advantages of your start-up's tools and services to build trust and credibility with potential clients.

In summary, the increasing global demand for disaster management and risk prediction solutions is expected to drive the success of a start-up that can deliver innovative tools and services. By undertaking the necessary steps, including validating the business idea, building a robust product, assembling a strong team, securing funding, establishing strategic partnerships, and developing an effective marketing strategy, the start-up will be well-positioned for success in the year 2024 and beyond.

Virtual Reality Art Galleries

In 2024, the virtual reality (VR) landscape has evolved significantly, making it the perfect time for launching a cutting-edge VR art gallery start-up business. This summary discusses the primary factors contributing to the potential success of this business and outlines the fundamental steps required to get started.

Key Factors:

1. **Market Demand**: The COVID-19 pandemic left a lasting impact on how people interact with the arts. As people seek to overcome geographical barriers and maintain safety measures while enjoying cultural experiences, virtual art galleries have evolved into a sought-after solution. Beyond the changes driven by the global health crisis, VR experiences offer unmatched accessibility and immersive experiences. These factors all contribute to an increasing market demand for state-of-the-art VR art platforms.

2. **Enhanced VR Technology**: Recent advancements in VR technology have dramatically improved the user experience. Next-gen headsets and peripherals provide users with more realistic graphics, improved haptic feedback, and a seamless interface. High-speed internet connections also enable smoother streaming and lag-free browsing, thus ensuring accessibility and convenience for users across the globe.

3. **Revenue Models**: Running a VR art gallery start-up presents a plethora of revenue generation opportunities. From charging art institutions and artists for exhibition space to offering subscription-based access to exclusive collections, various business models can be explored to ensure profitability.

To Get Started with a VR Art Gallery Business in 2024, Follow These Essential Steps:

1. **Market Research**: Understanding customer expectations, interests, and habits is vital when trying to tailor the offerings to the target audience. Conduct thorough market research to gather valuable insights and data regarding trends, preferences, and competitor analysis.

2. **Product Development**: Leverage cutting-edge VR technology and collaborate with industry experts to create an immersive, user-friendly platform that suits the varying needs of both artists and art enthusiasts, while standing out from competitors.

3. **Partnership Building**: Forge strategic partnerships within the art industry by connecting with museums, art festivals, galleries, and artists who would benefit from sharing their works within the VR platform. Collaborations with educational institutions and emerging artists can further help expand your audience reach.

4. **Marketing and Branding**: Create a strong brand identity, marketing campaigns, and a striking online presence. Social media, art forums, and targeted advertising are essential for promoting the VR art gallery and creating a buzz around new exhibitions and events. Utilizing influencer marketing among the art community is another effective method for increasing awareness and credibility.

5. **Legal Considerations and Funding**: Secure necessary permits and copyrights before launching and consult with legal advisors to understand any liabilities or contractual requirements, such as user privacy and data protection. Additionally, explore funding options, such as venture capital investments, crowdfunding, or grants to get the business off the ground and keep it running smoothly.

In conclusion, the advancements in VR technology, the shift in consumer preferences, and the rising demand for accessible, immersive art experiences make 2024 an ideal time to establish a successful VR art gallery start-up. By following the steps outlined above, entrepreneurs and visionaries can contribute to the growth of art appreciation within an increasingly connected and borderless world.

AI-Generated Music and Art Platforms

In recent years, the demand for personalized, dynamic, and interactive artistic experiences has been on the rise. As we approach 2024, consumers crave more innovative and tailored content in music and art. This is where an AI-generated music and art platform can prosper. Such a start-up will leverage the power of artificial intelligence to create an engaging, customizable, and accessible experience for users, opening up a new world of possibilities for the creative industry.

Why Would an AI-Generated Music and Art Platform be Successful in 2024?

1. **Personalization**: Consumers will be drawn to the unique offerings of an AI-generated music and art platform as it can deliver personalized experiences based on individual preferences.

2. **AI Advancements**: Rapidly advancing AI and machine-learning technologies will provide the backbone for the platform, generating high-quality content that is both novel and engaging.

3. **Time Efficiency**: AI-generated music and art provide a quick and efficient way to access creative content, making it appealing to users who face time constraints.

4. **Collaboration Opportunities**: The platform will allow artists, musicians, and creators to collaborate in new ways, making it more attractive to upcoming talents.

5. **Untapped Market Potential**: Although there are existing AI-generated art and music platforms, the market still has room for disruptive new entrants providing unique features and experiences.

Steps to Get Started:

1. **Market Research**: Conduct extensive research to understand the target audience, competitors, and identify potential gaps in the market. Evaluate the demand for AI-generated music and art, and identify ways to differentiate the platform from existing offerings.

2. **Assemble a Team**: Build a strong team comprising experts in artificial intelligence, programming, music, art, and other relevant fields. This diverse

group will contribute to creating a platform that caters to the evolving needs of creative professionals and consumers alike.

3. **Develop a Unique AI Algorithm**: Begin by developing a proprietary AI algorithm that generates music and art according to user preferences, input, and data. This unique technology should offer adaptive and evolving outputs that stand out from existing solutions in the market.

4. **Platform Design and Development**: Construct a user-friendly and intuitive platform that seamlessly integrates AI-generated music and art with robust features such as customization, collaboration, and sharing capabilities.

5. **Funding and Partnership**: Secure funding from investors, venture capitalists or crowdfunding sources, ensuring adequate resources for platform development, marketing, and future growth. Additionally, seek partnerships with established creators, musicians, influencers, and stakeholders in the art and music industries to enhance credibility and expand your potential user base.

6. **Launch and Marketing Strategy**: Launch the platform with a carefully crafted marketing strategy that highlights its unique features, leverages social media, and appeals to the target demographics. Offer incentives like early adopter deals or exclusive access to attract users and encourage word-of-mouth promotion.

7. **Continuous Improvement and Expansion**: Gather user feedback and data to continuously improve the platform and its algorithms, ensuring that it stays relevant and innovative. Explore potential collaborations, expansions into new markets or niches, and develop additional revenue streams, such as offering premium features, subscriptions or licensing opportunities.

By leveraging the power of AI, personalization, and efficient content creation, an AI-generated music and art platform can capitalize on the growing demand for innovative artistic experiences in 2024. The key to success lies in building a user-centric platform with strong technological foundations, strategic marketing, and continuous improvement, ensuring long-term growth and sustainability for the start-up.

Gig Economy Job Platforms

A gig economy job platform start-up in 2024 is poised for success due to changing workforce dynamics, the growing demand for flexible work, rising adoption of digital technology, and improved platform offerings. To capitalize on this opportunity, founders must take certain steps, such as identifying market niches, conducting market research, forming the right team, building a robust platform, and implementing effective marketing and monetization strategies.

The gig economy has been on the rise, characterized by temporary, short-term, and independent work arrangements. As we approach 2024, a gig economy job platform start-up has immense potential for success, driven by various socio-economic and technological factors.

Reasons for Success in 2024:

1. **Changing Workforce Dynamics**: Globalization, remote work, and a preference for work-life balance make gig work more appealing to both businesses and workers. The younger demographic, particularly Gen Z and Millennials, tend to value flexibility and variety in their work, providing opportunities for gig economy platforms.

2. **Economic Factors**: The world economy is becoming more unpredictable, with many sectors experiencing disruptions due to technological advancements or other unforeseen circumstances. Businesses are increasingly seeking ways to cut costs, optimize resources, and maintain flexibility, which has led to an increased demand for gig workers.

3. **Advancements in Digital Technology**: The adoption of digital and mobile technology and the ubiquity of the internet have made it easier for workers and businesses to connect and collaborate. A gig economy job platform start-up can capitalize on these advancements to provide an efficient and user-friendly experience for all parties.

4. **Improved Platform Offerings**: By 2024, the start-up can benefit from lessons learned in the past by predecessors and competitors. Better matching algorithms, seamless communication features, improved user experience, and enhanced trust protocols can be implemented to redefine industry expectations.

To Launch a Successful Gig Economy Job Platform Start-Up, the Following Steps Should be Considered:

1. **Identify Market Niche**: Determine the specific market segment and services to be offered. This could include professional services, creative services, maintenance services, or any other area with potential for temporary or freelance work.

2. **Conduct Market Research**: Evaluate traditional and gig economy competitors to better understand the market landscape and identify any gaps or opportunities for differentiation.

3. **Build the Right Team**: Assemble a team with diverse expertise in technology, user experience, marketing, and operations to develop and manage the platform.

4. **Develop a Robust Platform**: Build a platform that incorporates advanced matching algorithms, user-friendly interfaces, and security measures to ensure trust, reliability, and seamless communication between workers and businesses.

5. **Implement Effective Marketing Strategies**: Create a marketing plan that utilizes digital channels such as social media, content marketing, and search engine optimization to attract businesses and gig workers to the platform.

6. **Determine Monetization Models**: Explore various monetization avenues, such as a commission-based structure, subscription fees, or premium services, ensuring all parties perceive value in the platform's offerings.

The gig economy has been growing consistently, and as we approach 2024, the demand for reliable and efficient gig economy job platforms is expected to increase. Following the basic steps of identifying a market niche, building a diverse team, developing a robust platform, and implementing effective marketing and monetization strategies can significantly contribute to the success of a gig economy job platform start-up.

Healthcare, Wellness, and Fitness

AI-Driven Health Care Services

As the world continues to embrace the ever-evolving innovations of artificial intelligence, the health care domain in 2024 is no exception. An AI-Driven health care services start-up holds immense potential for success, given the increasing need for efficiency, accuracy, and cost-effectiveness in medical services. By leveraging sophisticated algorithms and big data analysis techniques, AI-driven businesses have the potential to revolutionize the delivery of health care services.

Factors Contributing to Success:

1. **Personalized Medicine and Diagnostics**: AI-driven health care services can provide personalized medicine and diagnostics with unprecedented precision by analyzing individual genomic data and lifestyle factors.

2. **Telehealth Expansion**: Remote monitoring, telemedicine consultations, and the use of wearable devices have gained significant traction during the COVID-19 pandemic. AI-driven platforms can further push this trend by offering efficient virtual medical services.

3. **Big Data and Improved Patient Care**: The analysis of health care data, like electronic health records and medical imaging, can support clinical decision-making by providing accurate and predictive insights.

4. **Artificial Intelligence-Enabled Drug Discovery**: AI-driven platforms can accelerate the drug discovery process, reduce costs, and make it quicker for new pharmaceutical breakthroughs to reach patients.

5. **Cost Reduction and Increased Efficiency**: By reducing redundancies, automating administrative tasks, and optimizing workflows, AI can increase efficiency and have a positive impact on the overall costs of health care services.

Basic Steps for Starting an AI-Driven Health Care Services Start-Up:

1. **Idea Validation**: Conduct thorough market research on the health care domain and existing AI applications to identify gaps and growth potential.

2. **Defining the Niche**: Determine the niche or specialization your start-up will focus on based on the market gap analysis. This will guide your entire product or service development.

3. **Building a Core Team**: Assemble a multidisciplinary team with expertise in artificial intelligence, machine learning, data analytics, and medical domain knowledge.

4. **Securing Essential Resources**: Obtain the necessary financial resources for starting the business, either through bootstrapping, investor funding, or partnership with established companies.

5. **Developing the AI-Driven Solution**: Work with your team to develop the AI-driven platform, product, or service, which will integrate various data sources, algorithms, machine learning models, and user interfaces.

6. **Regulatory Compliance**: Ensure compliance with legal, ethical, and regulatory standards for AI-driven health care innovations, such as data privacy and security.

7. **Crafting a Go-To-Market Strategy**: Develop a strategic marketing plan to create market awareness and adoption of the AI-driven health care services. It is essential to build relationships with key stakeholders, such as hospitals, health care providers, insurance companies, and patient advocacy groups.

8. **Continuous Improvement and Product Updates**: AI-driven solutions must be continually updated as the medical and AI fields develop. Ensuring your product or service remains relevant with evolving trends and maintains a competitive edge is crucial for long-term success.

The AI-driven health care services sector is poised for significant growth in 2024. By embracing this technology's disruptive potential and addressing specific gaps in the market, your start-up can harness this momentum for lasting success.

Personalized Nutrition Platforms

In 2024, starting a Personalized Nutrition Platform (PNP) start-up business holds immense potential for success, given the increasing demand for customized and data-driven nutrition solutions. To start a PNP business, it is essential to conduct market research, develop product offerings, build technology infrastructure, comply with regulatory requirements, establish a marketing and distribution strategy, and secure funding.

Rising Interest in Personalized Nutrition: Factors contributing to the growing interest in personalized nutrition include rising health awareness, increased understanding of individual nutritional needs, improvements in science and technology, and the growing popularity of wearable devices that monitor health and fitness parameters. As consumers increasingly search for customized, engaging, and effective nutrition solutions, PNP businesses that offer tailored nutrition advice and meal planning services will find extensive market opportunities.

Steps to Start a Personalized Nutrition Platform Start-up Business:

1. **Market Research and Analysis**: Conduct in-depth research on the personalized nutrition industry and analyze market trends, consumer requirements, and your competition. Be aware of upcoming trends in technology and identify previously unmet nutritional demands that could be addressed with personalized solutions.

2. **Define Product Offerings**: Outline the product offerings that suit your target audience, including meal planning, customized diets, nutrition counseling, or supplements. Determine if you will focus on specific dietary preferences or target particular health conditions, such as weight loss, sports nutrition, or diabetes management.

3. **Technology Infrastructure and Development**: Develop a user-friendly, data-driven platform that will allow users to input their personal information, preferences, and health goals. The platform should be designed to analyze this data using artificial intelligence or machine learning algorithms, then create personalized nutrition plans and deliver actionable insights to users. Consider building mobile applications for Android and iOS systems to make your services easily accessible to a wide audience.

4. **Regulatory Compliance and Data Privacy**: Ensure that your business adheres to relevant food, supplement, and data privacy regulations. Consult with a legal advisor to help navigate the regulatory landscape and protect your customers' data privacy.

5. **Marketing and Distribution Strategy**: Create a marketing plan that targets your core audience and utilizes modern marketing techniques such as social media, content marketing, influencer collaborations, and search engine optimization. Consider partnering with health clubs, wellness centers, and medical professionals to increase your distribution channels.

6. **Funding and Financial Planning**: Secure the necessary funding to start the business, which can include self-funding, seeking investors, or applying for grants and loans. Develop a financial plan to project revenue, costs, and profitability in the initial years of the business.

In conclusion, a personalized nutrition platform start-up business can thrive in 2024 due to the growing demand for specialized and data-driven nutrition solutions. To ensure success, it is imperative to address all steps, including rigorous market research, developing a comprehensive product offering, establishing a technology infrastructure, complying with regulations, creating an effective marketing and distribution strategy, and securing the necessary funding.

JAIME GEHLY

Mental Health Chatbot Services

A Mental Health Chatbot Services start-up business is poised for success in 2024 due to a strong demand for mental health support, advances in AI technology, and growing acceptance of digital mental health solutions. To ensure the successful launch and growth of the business, aspiring entrepreneurs should consider the following basic steps: market research and validation, product development, regulatory compliance, establishing partnerships, marketing and scaling the business.

Key Factors:

1. **Growing Demand for Mental Health Support**: In 2024, the world continues to face unprecedented challenges, including the residual effects of the COVID-19 pandemic, climate change, political instability, and growing economic inequality. Consequently, the demand for mental health services has skyrocketed, leaving traditional therapy services overburdened and unable to meet this demand. A mental health chatbot service provides accessible, affordable, and private mental health support, positioning it perfectly to meet this increasing need.

2. **Advances in AI Technology**: Technological advancements, including the development of advanced AI language models such as GPT-4, have made it possible for chatbots to engage dynamically with users, understand context, and provide empathetic and personalized support. Leveraging these cutting-edge AI technologies, mental health chatbot services can deliver valuable mental health assistance, augmenting limited human resources in the industry.

3. **Growing Acceptance of Digital Mental Health Solutions**: The widespread adoption of telemedicine, online counseling, and other remote mental health tools in the wake of the COVID-19 pandemic has helped normalize digital mental health solutions. Given that people are increasingly comfortable with technology-based mental health support, a start-up in the chatbot services space is strategically placed to capitalize on this trend.

Basic Steps to Get Started:

1. **Conduct Market Research and Validation**: Thorough market research is fundamental for understanding the needs and pain points of potential users. By identifying the target audience, validating demand, and exploring competitors in the digital mental health space, entrepreneurs can pinpoint unique selling propositions and ensure greater success for their start-up.

2. **Develop the Chatbot Product**: The product development phase involves creating a chatbot that is user-friendly, empathetic, and adaptable. Developing such a tool requires a multidisciplinary team, including AI developers, designers, and mental health professionals, to ensure an evidence-based and ethically grounded solution.

3. **Ensure Regulatory Compliance and Ethics**: Mental health chatbot services must comply with relevant regulations and privacy laws, such as HIPAA and GDPR, to ensure the secure handling of sensitive information. Additionally, the start-up should establish ethical guidelines and safeguarding protocols to address potential risks associated with AI-based interventions.

4. **Establish Collaborative Partnerships**: Form strategic alliances with established mental health organizations, academic institutions, and healthcare providers to foster credibility, secure expert consultation, and facilitate pilot testing and service integration.

5. **Marketing and Scaling the Business**: Once the chatbot service is ready for launch, execute a comprehensive marketing and public relations campaign to raise awareness and drive user adoption. Identify key performance indicators to track, and continuously iterate the chatbot in response to user feedback and advancements in AI technology.

In conclusion, a Mental Health Chatbot Services start-up is well-positioned for success in 2024, provided it is grounded in comprehensive market research, employs advanced AI technologies, and operates ethically and in compliance with appropriate regulations. By addressing the pressing need for accessible and affordable mental health support, this venture can thrive in a rapidly evolving digital landscape.

Telemedicine Platforms

In 2024, the telemedicine platform sector is a thriving market and a promising start-up business opportunity due to various factors. The ongoing advancements in technology, the increasing adoption of telemedicine, the growing need for patient-centric healthcare, pandemic-driven changes, cost-effectiveness, and government support are pushing the telemedicine industry towards unprecedented growth. Aspiring entrepreneurs can delve into this market and establish a successful start-up by following the basic steps outlined below.

Telemedicine Adoption in 2024: In recent years, telemedicine platforms have transformed the healthcare landscape, resulting in widespread adoption by healthcare providers and patients alike. The global pandemic has further accelerated telemedicine's growth, emphasizing the need for accessible, efficient, and safe healthcare consultations. As a consequence, telemedicine platforms will continue to be an integral part of the healthcare industry in 2024, providing a range of services such as remote consultation, monitoring, prescription management, and mental health support, among others.

Factors Contributing to Telemedicine Platform Success:

1. **Technological Advancements**: The rapid development of technologies such as 5G, IoT, artificial intelligence, and machine learning has enabled telemedicine platforms to provide seamless virtual consultations, accurate diagnoses, and better patient outcomes.

2. **Patient-Centric Healthcare**: The shift towards patient-centric care calls for increased accessibility, comfort, and convenience. Telemedicine platforms offer patients the flexibility to connect with healthcare providers from the comfort of their homes, making it an appealing option.

3. **Pandemic-Driven Changes**: The COVID-19 pandemic has accelerated the digital transformation of healthcare systems worldwide. Telemedicine platforms have become a critical tool in managing healthcare services, particularly for high-risk populations, during infectious disease outbreaks.

4. **Cost-Effectiveness**: Telemedicine platforms streamline processes, reduce transportation costs, and minimize the need for physical infrastructure, resulting in cost savings for both patients and providers.

5. **Government Support**: Governments worldwide have recognized telemedicine's potential and are providing regulatory support, funding, and incentives to promote the industry's growth.

Basic Steps to Establish a Telemedicine Start-up:

1. **Conduct Market Research**: Understand the target audience, competition, and market trends. Identify the segment in which the start-up will operate, such as primary care, mental health, or chronic disease management.

2. **Develop a Business Plan**: Create a comprehensive business plan outlining the start-up's goals, target audience, service offerings, revenue model, marketing strategy, and key milestones.

3. **Regulatory Compliance**: Familiarize yourself with and adhere to the pertinent telemedicine regulations, healthcare laws, and data privacy policies across different jurisdictions to ensure legal compliance.

4. **Develop the Telemedicine Platform**: Collaborate with experienced developers to create a user-friendly, secure, and HIPAA-compliant telemedicine platform, integrating features such as video conferencing, electronic health records, prescription management, and appointment scheduling.

5. **Assemble a Qualified Team**: Recruit experienced medical professionals, IT specialists, and administrative staff to ensure the platform's smooth functioning and maintain high-quality service offerings.

6. **Engage in Strategic Partnerships**: Network with healthcare providers, insurance companies, government agencies, and other stakeholders to gain support, drive user adoption, and increase credibility.

7. **Implement a Marketing Strategy**: Deploy digital marketing strategies, such as search engine optimization (SEO), social media marketing, and content marketing, to raise brand awareness and attract prospective users.

In conclusion, telemedicine platforms represent a promising and lucrative start-up venture in the 2024 healthcare landscape. By leveraging the right strategies, a telemedicine start-up can capitalize on the industry's rapid growth and secure long-term success.

Mental Wellness Apps

The growth of the mental wellness app industry is set to continue its upward trajectory in 2024, making it an increasingly attractive business opportunity for start-ups. Contributing factors include growing awareness around mental health, advancements in technology, the lasting effects of the COVID-19 pandemic, and a shift towards remote mental healthcare. Start-ups in this space can expect to see high demand and profitability for their products by following the basic steps of market analysis, app development, and effective marketing.

Key Factors:

Growing Awareness around Mental Health: Mental health issues have become a global crisis, affecting millions of people annually. In recent years, there has been a significant increase in public awareness, leading to the destigmatization of mental health conditions. This growing awareness has translated into a demand for mental wellness services including therapy, counseling, and digital solutions.

Advancements in Technology and Remote Healthcare: Technological advancements and increased smartphone penetration have allowed for easier access to mental health resources. Moreover, the growing acceptance of teleconferencing and remote healthcare options has further boosted the demand for mental wellness apps. These apps provide the users with tools such as mood tracking, stress relief exercises, meditation, and even personalized therapy sessions.

Impact of COVID-19 Pandemic: The coronavirus pandemic has increased stress and anxiety among individuals, leading to an upsurge in the demand for mental health support. As people have had to adapt to living and working remotely, they have sought out digital solutions to deal with the change. Mental wellness apps have become an attractive choice as they offer convenient, personalized, and affordable options to address the various mental health challenges people face.

Basic Steps to Get Started:

1. **Market Analysis and Idea Validation**: Conduct a comprehensive market analysis, studying the demographics and psychographics of the target audience, and identify potential competitors. Validate the unique selling proposition (USP) of your mental wellness app, ensuring it meets the needs of your target market and stands out in the competitive landscape.

2. **Plan a Scalable Business Model**: Determine your revenue model, whether it be through app sales, subscriptions, ads, or in-app purchases. Consider partnerships with therapists, healthcare providers, or other relevant organizations to enhance your offerings.

3. **App Development**: Hire a skilled team of developers, designers, and mental health experts for creating a user-friendly and visually appealing app with evidence-based practices. Ensure all the content provided caters to the different mental health needs of your market segment.

4. **Compliance and Regulations**: Comply with all applicable regulations and legal requirements, including seeking approvals or licenses from relevant professional bodies. Pay attention to privacy and data protection laws, especially when it comes to dealing with sensitive user information.

5. **Launching and Marketing**: Develop a comprehensive marketing plan, focusing on social media channels, targeted content, and public relations campaigns. Utilize influencers, reviews, and success stories to drive user engagement and increase brand exposure.

6. **Continuous Improvement and Growth**: Monitor user feedback, make necessary improvements, and frequently update features within the app to stay relevant in the market. Be prepared to adapt to industry innovations, and customers' evolving needs to promote long-term user retention and profitability.

In conclusion, a mental wellness app start-up focusing on addressing the growing demand for remote healthcare, providing personalized solutions, and catering to diverse mental health needs is poised for immense success and profitability in 2024. The start-up must follow a strategic approach, adhering to basic steps like market analysis, app development, marketing, and continuous improvement to guarantee a prosperous venture in this booming industry.

Art Therapy Platforms

In 2024, establishing an art therapy platform start-up is a wise and lucrative choice for several reasons. With increasing awareness of mental health issues, a growing acceptance of alternative therapies, advances in technology, and an expanding remote work culture, art therapy platforms can provide accessible and effective means for comprehensive mental well-being. In order to launch a successful art therapy platform, entrepreneurs must follow some basic steps: market and product research, creating a business plan, assembling the right team, building a digital platform, and promoting the business.

Reasons for Success:

1. **Greater Awareness of Mental Health Issues**: Society is putting more emphasis on addressing mental health issues now than ever before. As a result, there is a growing demand for accessible and innovative mental health solutions. An online art therapy platform offers an unconstrained and creative approach to self-expression and healing, catering to a larger audience seeking mental well-being.

2. **Acceptance of Alternative Therapies**: As people become more open to alternative therapies, art therapy is gaining recognition and acceptance for its therapeutic value. An online platform will be able to reach more people, enabling them to benefit from art therapy's healing potential, regardless of location or background.

3. **Technological Advances**: In 2024, technology plays a crucial role in making art therapy platforms practical and effective. With high-speed internet, video streaming, and virtual reality tools, users can explore their thoughts and emotions through a variety of creative and interactive digital formats. As technology continues to improve, the market for online art therapy will grow.

4. **Remote Work Culture**: More people work remotely in 2024 than ever before, which creates a need for unique solutions to manage stress and work-life balance. An art therapy platform can effectively target this expanding remote workforce, by providing convenient, flexible, and accessible self-care options.

Basic Steps to Get Started:

1. **Market and Product Research**: Begin by conducting market research to identify target customers, their needs, and the opportunities present in the industry. Also, explore different types of art therapy practices and understand the online resources and tools needed to seamlessly provide these services.

2. **Create a Business Plan**: Develop a detailed business plan to outline start-up costs, target audience, revenue goals, marketing strategies, and technological requirements. This will help organize your resources and serve as a blueprint for the growth of your business.

3. **Assemble the Right Team**: Hire skilled professionals with experience in art therapy, technology, design, and marketing. These individuals will help develop and execute the business plan and ensure its success.

4. **Build a Digital Platform**: Invest in the development of a user-friendly online platform, incorporating a variety of art therapy tools, resources, and virtual sessions. Incorporate high-quality video and audio streaming options, as well as advanced security features to protect user privacy and data.

5. **Promote the Business**: Implement marketing strategies to promote your art therapy platform, including social media campaigns, content marketing, and collaborations with healthcare professionals, non-profit organizations, and educational institutions. By raising awareness and establishing partnerships, you can increase your platform's visibility and success.

In conclusion, the combination of societal changes, technology advancements, and the growth of remote work in 2024 present the perfect opportunity to launch a successful art therapy platform. By following the basic steps mentioned above, entrepreneurs can create a thriving start-up in this high-demand industry.

Adaptive Therapy Management

In the constantly evolving healthcare landscape, an adaptive therapy management startup presents a well-informed and forward-looking business prospect in 2024. As the challenges of psychiatric and cognitive health disorders continue to grow globally, there is an increasing need for personalized, adaptive, and scalable treatment solutions. By harnessing cutting-edge technology, data analysis, and evidence-based practices, this venture has immense potential to revolutionize mental healthcare management and generate strong growth.

Reasons for Success:

1. **Addressing a Growing Need**: The prevalence of mental health issues has never been greater, and the COVID-19 pandemic has further exacerbated these challenges. Consequently, there is a high demand for innovative and accessible mental healthcare services, and an adaptive therapy startup can capitalize on this opportunity.

2. **Leveraging Advances in Technology**: The ongoing development of Artificial Intelligence (AI), machine learning, and big data analytics allows for more accurate predictive models and personalized treatments, ensuring better health outcomes for patients. An adaptive therapy management startup can make the most of these technological advancements to develop targeted and effective therapeutic interventions.

3. **Embracing Telemedicine and Remote Services**: Social distancing norms and growing acceptance of digital platforms have reinforced the need for telemedicine and remote service offerings. A startup in the adaptive therapy management space has the flexibility to tap into this developing trend and provide patients with convenient and secure access to therapy wherever they are.

4. **Expanding Scope for Collaboration and Partnerships**: Opportunities abound for strategic partnerships and collaborations in research, technology, and distribution. These alliances can provide the startup with additional resources and scalability, fast-tracking its growth.

To Launch an Adaptive Therapy Management Startup, the Following Basic Steps Should be Followed:

1. **Identify a Market Gap**: Analyze the mental healthcare landscape and determine the needs that are not being addressed by existing services. This assessment will serve as the foundation for your startup's value proposition.

2. **Develop a Business Plan**: Clearly outline your objectives, strategies for growth, target market, and how you plan to address their needs. Detail the resources required, projected revenues, and risk mitigation measures.

3. **Assemble a Talented and Diverse Team**: Recruit a multidisciplinary team that includes qualified mental health professionals, technology experts, and experienced business leaders. This will ensure a balanced blend of clinical and technological expertise, resulting in innovative and impactful solutions.

4. **Establish a Technology Infrastructure**: Invest in advanced systems and tools, such as AI and big data analytics, that can process and analyze real-time patient data. This will enable the development of personalized treatment plans that adapt to the patients' changing needs.

5. **Secure Funding**: Explore various funding opportunities, such as venture capital, angel investments, and crowdfunding campaigns, to raise the necessary resources to develop and scale your startup.

6. **Collaborate and Partner**: Proactively initiate and pursue collaborations and partnerships with healthcare providers, research institutions, and technology companies to expand your network and share resources.

7. **Regulatory Compliance and Ethical Considerations**: Be aware of and adhere to the legal and ethical regulations pertaining to patient care, data privacy, and digital health solutions.

8. **Market and Promote Your Startup**: Develop a comprehensive marketing strategy that highlights your startup's unique strengths and advantages. Communicate the benefits of personalized, adaptive therapy to potential clients, healthcare professionals, and investors.

In summary, an adaptive therapy management startup has significant potential for success in 2024. Backed by advanced technology, data-driven insights, and a scalable business model, it has the capability to make a profound impact on the mental health landscape and revolutionize the way therapy is delivered and accessed.

DNA-Based Skincare and Wellness Solutions

The rapidly evolving personal care market, fueled by increasing consumer awareness on wellness, skincare, and the pursuit of a personalized approach, presents a unique opportunity for the emergence of successful and highly profitable start-ups. In 2024, a DNA-based skincare and wellness solutions company will thrive due to advanced technology, widespread access to personal genotype data, and growing demand for customized consumer products.

Key Success Factors:

1. **Personalized Approach**: By leveraging DNA-based insights, the start-up will create tailored skincare and wellness plans solutions that cater to individual consumer needs, enhancing effectiveness and customer satisfaction.

2. **Advanced Technology**: Technological improvements in genomic sequencing, data processing, and bioinformatics enable the company to analyze consumer DNA rapidly and cost-effectively, making it a viable commercial endeavor.

3. **Informed Choices**: Consumer access to their genetic information will empower them to make informed decisions on their skincare and wellness regimens, providing a competitive advantage for the start-up's DNA-based solutions.

4. **Market Trends**: A rising preference for natural and clean beauty products, as well as an increasing focus on preventative care and self-care, create a conducive market environment for the start-up.

Basic Steps to Get Started:

1. **Market Research and Analysis**: Conduct comprehensive research on the skincare and wellness industry, obtaining insights into the target audience, key competitors, and market trends.

2. **Product Development**: Collaborate with geneticists, dermatologists, and bioinformatics experts to develop a range of customized skincare and wellness products based on genetic profiles.

3. **Intellectual Property and Legal Framework**: Secure patents for unique technologies and formulations, and ensure compliance with relevant regulations, such as data privacy and product safety.

4. **Strategic Partnerships**: Establish relationships with reputable laboratories, manufacturers, and distributors, which will be essential for successful product development, production, and supply chain management.

5. **Brand Development**: Invest in branding efforts to communicate the unique value proposition of DNA-based skincare and wellness solutions, creating a compelling and memorable visual identity.

6. **Online Presence**: Develop an e-commerce platform and a robust digital marketing strategy to reach the target market, utilizing social media, SEO, and influencers to drive consumer engagement and sales.

7. **Proof of Concept**: Roll out a pilot program to assess the efficacy of the products, refine formulations, and gather testimonials to build credibility and trust.

The combination of a personalized approach, cutting-edge technology, increasing consumer awareness, and favorable market trends make a DNA-based skincare and wellness solutions start-up a highly profitable venture in 2024. By following the outlined steps, a start-up can successfully launch and meet the growing demand for customized and science-driven beauty products, carving out its own niche in the industry.

JAIME GEHLY

Neurotech Solutions

The neurotechnology industry is projected to experience substantial growth in the next few years, with a widespread range of applications and potential impact on various sectors. A neurotech solutions start-up in 2024 would be an ideal business venture, considering the increasing demand for innovative technologies that can enhance human capabilities and improve mental health and well-being. Entrepreneurs aiming to enter this market must follow several crucial steps to launch a successful start-up in this promising sector.

Market Opportunities: The advancements in neuroscience and exponential growth of AI (artificial intelligence) have paved the way for groundbreaking innovations in Neurotech. This industry focuses on technology that connects with the human brain, directing applications in neurorehabilitation, cognitive enhancement, and mental health solutions. Key drivers for the neurotech market include:

1. **Aging Population**: With a globally aging population, the demand for solutions catering to age-related cognitive decline, memory loss, and other degenerative brain diseases, like Alzheimer's and Parkinson's, is on the rise.

2. **Mental Health**: According to the World Health Organization, mental health issues affect 1 in 4 people globally. The neurotech industry can provide effective, non-invasive solutions, ultimately improving mental healthcare access.

3. **Workforce Enhancement**: Businesses are always looking for ways to boost the productivity and capabilities of their workforce. Neurotech solutions can potentially maximize focus, creativity, and concentration, making it appealing to companies striving for a competitive edge.

Steps to Launch a Neurotech Solutions Start-up:

1. **Market Research**: Conduct a thorough analysis of the neurotech industry, identify key players, understand current trends, determine market gaps, and pinpoint the targeted customer segments.

2. **Unique Value Proposition**: Develop a clear pitch stating how the start-up's neurotech solutions will differentiate from competitors. Address issues like usability, scalability, affordability, and innovation for a successful value proposition.

3. **Business Plan**: Create a comprehensive business plan outlining the mission, vision, target market, product roadmap, team requirements, financial projections, marketing strategy, partnership opportunities, and an exit strategy.

4. **Legal Requirements**: Establish the start-up legally as a business entity. Consult legal professionals to ensure compliance with relevant regulations, including data privacy and medical device regulations.

5. **Product Development**: Prototype and continually iterate the neurotech solutions, ensuring products meet industry standards and address the needs of the target market. Establish partnerships with other industry players for access to cutting-edge technology or resources.

6. **Funding**: Identify and secure sources of funding, such as venture capital, angel investment, or government grants for research and development.

7. **Marketing Strategy**: Develop a detailed go-to-market strategy by identifying the key customer channels, focusing on digital and social media marketing campaigns, attending industry events, leveraging strategic partnerships, and utilizing PR efforts.

8. **Team Building**: Assemble a team of skilled professionals, including neuroscientists, engineers, software developers, and business experts who share the same vision and commitment to excellence.

9. **Continuous Improvement**: Regularly gather and analyze data on the product's performance, customer satisfaction, and market trends to inform critical adjustments to the strategy, products, or business model.

In conclusion, a neurotech solutions start-up in 2024 presents an excellent opportunity due to the immense potential of this cutting-edge industry.

Personalized Genomics and Medicine

A personalized genomics and medicine start-up has the potential to become a highly profitable and innovative business in 2024. With advancements in genetics and biotechnology, this start-up will cater to the growing demand for personalized healthcare solutions. Personalized genomics involves the study of an individual's genetic makeup to create customized medical treatments, disease prevention plans, and lifestyle recommendations. The following benefits and basic steps to get started highlight the promising nature of this business.

Benefits:

1. **Rising Healthcare Costs**: The healthcare industry faces a constant challenge to reduce costs, and personalized medicine can help by targeting treatments more effectively, potentially reducing hospitalizations and long-term care expenses.

2. **Technological Advancements**: State-of-the-art tools like next-generation sequencing, bioinformatics, and gene editing have made it increasingly affordable to decode and understand the human genome, driving the rapid expansion of personalized genomics and medicine.

3. **Improved Treatment Outcomes**: Personalized medicine is expected to dramatically enhance treatment effectiveness by tailoring therapies and drugs to an individual's genetic profile, reducing trial-and-error treatments, and minimizing adverse drug reactions.

4. **Preventative Medicine**: Identifying genetic predispositions to diseases can help in guiding prevention plans for individuals, promoting healthier lifestyles, and efficient resource allocation for public health programs.

5. **Consumer Interest**: Growing consumer awareness of genomic information and its implications on health leads to increased demand for access to such information and the development of customized healthcare plans.

Steps to Get Started:

1. **Business Plan**: Develop a comprehensive business plan highlighting your unique value proposition, target market, revenue streams, budget, and growth strategy.

2. **Strategic Partnerships**: Collaborate with biotechnology and research facilities, hospitals, and healthcare providers to access the latest technology and research.

3. **Required Certifications and Permits**: Obtain necessary certifications, licenses, and permits for operating a genomics and medicine start-up, ensuring compliance with health and data protection regulations.

4. **Intellectual Property Protection**: Register patents, trademarks, and copyrights to protect your discoveries on gene-based treatments, unique algorithms, or any other proprietary innovations.

5. **Technology Infrastructure**: Develop scalable and secure IT systems for processing genomic data, employing bioinformaticians and data scientists to analyze and interpret the results.

6. **Funding and Investment**: Secure funding from investors, government grants, or crowd-funding campaigns to cover start-up costs and support ongoing research and development.

7. **Marketing and Brand Visibility**: Create a strong online presence through social media, content marketing, and targeted advertising campaigns to educate the public on the benefits of personalized genomics and medicine.

8. **Ethical Considerations**: Develop guidelines and policies addressing privacy concerns about personal genomic information, ensuring data collection and storage practices adhere to relevant laws.

9. **Quality and Performance Metrics**: Establish quality and performance metrics to evaluate the start-up's success and the effectiveness of treatments, ensuring data-driven decision-making and continuous improvement.

By focusing on these advantages and action steps, a personalized genomics and medicine start-up can capitalize on the opportunities presented in 2024, significantly benefiting both patients and the healthcare industry.

Smart Fitness Wearables

A Smart Fitness Wearables start-up business would be a good choice in 2024 due to the increasing demand for wearable technology and the growing trend of health and fitness awareness. With technological advancements, people prefer to monitor their fitness levels using wearable devices, such as smartwatches, fitness trackers, and other related devices. Customers are willing to spend money on these devices to monitor their daily activities, measure their vital statistics, and track their workouts to achieve their fitness goals.

If You Are Interested in Starting a Smart Fitness Wearables Start-Up Business, Here are the Steps You Can Follow:

1. **Conduct Market Research**: Identify your target audience and competitors. Understand the needs and preferences of your target customers and what kind of products your competitors are offering.

2. **Develop Your Business Plan**: Include your financial projections, marketing strategies, and product development plan. Identify your budget, sales targets, and the resources you would need to achieve your goals.

3. **Choose Your Products and Suppliers**: Identify your product range, such as smartwatches, fitness trackers, heart rate monitors, and other devices. Partner with reliable suppliers and manufacturers that can deliver quality products at a reasonable price.

4. **Develop Your Branding and Marketing Strategy**: Come up with a unique brand name, logo, and brand messaging that resonates with your target audience. Create a marketing plan that includes customer acquisition strategies, such as social media campaigns, influencer partnerships, and events.

5. **Build Your Online Presence**: Create an e-commerce website that showcases your products and allows customers to make purchases. Develop your social media presence to promote your brand, engage with your customers, and market your products.

6. **Launch Your Business**: Introduce your products to the market through social media, e-commerce platform, influencer partnerships, and other marketing channels. Continuously review your sales performance and adopt new strategies to improve your market share.

In summary, starting a Smart Fitness Wearables start-up business in 2024 has the potential to be a profitable venture due to the growing trend of health and fitness awareness. By conducting thorough market research and planning, developing quality products, implementing effective marketing strategies, and continuously reviewing your business performance can lead to success and revenue growth.

Mental Health Tracking and Support Platform

In 2024, the need for effective, accessible, and user-friendly mental health tracking and support platforms has become increasingly apparent. With a growing emphasis on mental health care and awareness, starting a mental health tracking and support platform as a business is an opportunity that answers market demands and provides immense value to millions of users worldwide.

Market Needs and Trends:

In recent years, mental health has gained recognition as an essential aspect of well-being. The increasing prevalence of mental health issues, the growing awareness of these conditions, and the insufficiency of traditional mental health care methods created a demand for innovative and accessible mental health support solutions. Technology, particularly mobile platforms and worldwide internet coverage, enables the development of robust mental health tracking and support platforms that help bridge the gap and cater to this need.

Competitive Advantage:

The competitive advantage of a mental health tracking and support platform lies in its ability to provide personalized, convenient, and affordable services that complement traditional mental health care approaches. Additionally, by utilizing advanced technologies such as Artificial Intelligence and Machine Learning, this platform can analyze data to predict patterns, recommend interventions, and continuously improve its services.

Basic Steps to Get Started:

1. **Market Research**: Understand the current mental health landscape, target audience, potential competitors, and identify service gaps to provide a unique and value-added solution.

2. **Business Plan**: Develop a comprehensive business plan outlining the platform's vision, mission, financial projections, market strategies, and other relevant aspects to ensure a successful start-up.

3. **Platform Development**: Collaborate with skilled developers, designers, psychologists, and other experts to create a user-friendly, secure, scalable, and reliable platform that supports mental health tracking and intervention services.

4. **Regulatory Compliance**: Adhere to local, regional, and international privacy laws, particularly those governing data protection and HIPAA. Ensure the platform complies with applicable mental health regulations as well.

5. **Secure Funding**: Apply for funding from investors, grants, or accelerator programs to finance platform development, marketing efforts, and ongoing operational costs.

6. **Assemble a Team**: Recruit and hire dedicated, skilled, and diverse professionals with expertise in mental health, technology, marketing, and business operations.

7. **Collaboration with Mental Health Professionals**: Partner with psychologists, psychiatrists, therapists, and other mental health professionals who will contribute their expertise to the platform and ensure the highest quality of support services.

8. **Marketing**: Develop targeted and effective marketing strategies to promote the platform, focusing on its unique selling points, benefits, and social impact. Leverage social media, content marketing, and other digital marketing channels.

9. **Launch and Iterate**: Soft-launch the platform, gather user feedback, and make continuous improvements. A comprehensive approach helps ensure the platform's success and its ability to serve its target audience effectively.

The growing awareness and demand for mental health support services position a mental health tracking and support platform as a high-impact business opportunity in 2024. By following the basic steps outlined above, the start-up can successfully navigate the competitive landscape and contribute positively to addressing the global mental health crisis.

Wearable Health Monitoring Devices

By 2024, the wearable health monitoring devices (WHMD) start-up industry is poised for success due to rapid advances in technology, increasing consumer interest, and the growing desire for personalized healthcare. A start-up in the WHMD sector can position itself for prosperity by carefully navigating the market, understanding consumer needs, and taking on the requisite steps and strategies. This document outlines the key reasons behind WHMD's rise to success in 2024 and the basics steps to establish a start-up.

Reasons For Success in 2024:

1. **Advancements in Technology**: With the continuous growth of IoT, AI, and sensor technology, WHMDs will be increasingly capable of monitoring and providing actionable insights to users. This enhances their appeal and will result in higher consumer adoption.

2. **Health Consciousness**: Society's increasing focus on well-being and disease prevention makes WHMDs popular, as users become more proactive in managing their health.

3. **Aging Population**: An older demographic requires greater availability and accessibility of healthcare. WHMDs offer the ability to monitor health conditions remotely, making them a cost-effective and convenient solution for an aging population.

4. **Rising Healthcare Costs**: Increasing costs for healthcare services will push people to invest in preventive measures, such as WHMDs, to maintain their health and save on long-term costs.

5. **Employer and Insurer Attraction**: Organizations and insurance companies are exploring options to incentivize healthy lifestyles or offer coverage for wearable devices, creating additional demand in the market.

Basic Steps to Start a WHMD Start-Up:

1. **Market Research**: Conduct thorough research to uncover untapped opportunities and identify the specific health monitoring needs of the target market.

2. **Unique Value Proposition**: Develop a unique value proposition by considering vital consumer concerns or identifying a niche that your product will address, such as tracking vital signs, monitoring specific health conditions, or encouraging active lifestyles.

3. **Product Design and Development**: Create a user-friendly, aesthetically appealing, and efficient wearable device that incorporates the latest technologies, such as AI or advanced sensors, to meet the consumer's health monitoring needs.

4. **Regulatory Compliance**: Obtain necessary certifications and follow regulatory guidelines for medical devices to ensure product safety and legal compliance.

5. **Intellectual Property Protection**: Secure patents or trademarks to ensure protection of the start-up's technology and unique features.

6. **Business Plan**: Develop a comprehensive business plan that includes market strategy, revenue projections, and operational tactics to secure funding and gauge the start-up's potential trajectory.

7. **Funding**: Seek investment from angel investors, venture capitalists, or government grants to finance your start-up and begin operations.

8. **Marketing and Sales**: Create a strong brand identity, develop promotional campaigns to raise awareness, and establish distribution channels such as online marketplaces, healthcare retailers, or partnerships with healthcare providers.

9. **Continuous Innovation**: Identify evolving consumer needs, emerging technologies, and upcoming trends to stay ahead of the competition and build an industry-leading WHMD start-up.

By taking these factors and steps into consideration, a WHMD start-up can position itself for success in the burgeoning market in 2024, ultimately contributing to a healthier population and thriving technology sector.

JAIME GEHLY

Nutrition and Fitness App Integrations

A Nutrition and Fitness App Integrations start-up business is poised for success in 2024 due to a myriad of factors including rising health awareness, a booming health & fitness industry, and technological advancements. This success can be achieved readily by following basic steps to kick-start the business.

In today's fast-paced world, people's concern for their health and well-being is constantly growing. With an increased emphasis on maintaining both physical and mental well-being, coupled with the prevalence of obesity and lifestyle-related diseases, the demand for fitness solutions has never been higher. In 2024, the stage has been set for a Nutrition and Fitness App Integrations start-up business to thrive.

Reasons for Success:

1. **Rising Health Awareness**: Improved understanding of the importance of a healthy lifestyle and better access to educational resources have contributed to the rising interest in nutrition and fitness in society. Consumers will welcome a platform that helps them maintain a balanced lifestyle and see tangible differences in their health and well-being.

2. **Booming Health & Fitness Industry**: The health & fitness market has seen exponential growth in recent years, with more people investing in workout equipment, gym memberships, personal training, and dietary supplements. In response, the development of fitness and nutrition apps has surged, indicating a sustainable and growing market for these services.

3. **Integrative Approach**: By integrating various nutrition, fitness, and health tracking apps, users will benefit from a unified and organized experience. This convenience is likely to encourage more people to utilize these services, leading to its widespread success.

4. **Technological Advancements**: Advanced AI and machine learning algorithms, when integrated into these apps, can help users receive personalized exercise routines and dietary recommendations. This hyper-focused approach dramatically increases user satisfaction and adherence to fitness goals.

Basic Steps to Get Started:

1. **Market Research**: Conduct comprehensive market analysis to identify the target demographic and successful competitors in the industry. Understand the current gaps in the market and analyze how your start-up can fill those needs.

2. **Develop a Unique Selling Proposition (USP)**: Based on your market research, create a USP that focuses on providing value to customers in a way that competitors don't. For example, easier integration, personalized recommendations, or a unique reward system.

3. **Develop the App**: Collaborate with a skilled development team to create a user-friendly, visually appealing, and efficient app. Utilize AI and machine learning capabilities for personalized recommendations and enhanced tracking.

4. **Acquire App Integrations**: Establish partnerships and collaborations with existing fitness and nutrition apps through API connections, for seamless interactivity and data transfer between apps.

5. **Create a Marketing Strategy**: Develop a multi-channel marketing campaign utilizing social media, search engine optimization, influencer partnerships, and targeted advertising to promote your business and reach your target audience.

6. **Secure Funding**: Approach venture capitalists or opt for crowdfunding to secure the initial investment for app development, marketing, and operational costs.

7. **Test and Launch**: Conduct beta testing and gather user feedback to make necessary adjustments before launching the final product. Receive feedback and data from the user base to continuously improve the app and its features.

By addressing the needs of the health-conscious population and leveraging advanced technology, a Nutrition and Fitness App Integrations start-up business has the potential to achieve significant success in 2024. Following these basic steps will lay the groundwork for a prosperous venture in this exciting and evolving market.

Community-Driven Wellness Platforms

In recent years, there has been a significant increase in consumer demand for wellness products, services, and personalized experiences. By 2024, a community-driven wellness platform start-up will greatly capitalize on this growth and yield impressive results. The platform will encourage users to lead a healthier lifestyle by connecting them to personalized wellness content, services, and communities based on their needs and preferences.

Market Potential:

1. **Increasing Wellness Consciousness**: The global wellness market has witnessed rapid growth and is estimated at a worth of $4.5 trillion. The rising popularity of holistic and preventive healthcare, coupled with a demand for personalized wellness experiences, signifies a significant opportunity for a community-driven platform.

2. **Consumer-Driven Healthcare**: Consumers are starting to take more control of their wellbeing and are looking for cohesive, user-friendly digital platforms that offer convenience, customization, and community support.

3. **Mental and Emotional Well-Being**: Wellness is not just about physical health but also mental and emotional health. Many people today struggle with stress, anxiety, and depression, making a community-driven platform an essential support mechanism.

Key Features for Success:

1. **Personalization**: Creating personalized wellness plans for individuals by collecting data through user profiles, questionnaires, and tracking tools, in addition to artificial intelligence and machine learning technologies.

2. **Collaboration**: Partnering with fitness and wellness professionals, mental health experts, nutritionists, and other industry professionals to provide diverse and high-quality content and services.

3. **Gamification and Rewards**: Incorporating gamification elements, such as progress tracking, badges, leaderboards, and rewards, to maintain user engagement and motivation.

4. **Scaling**: Developing mechanisms to handle growth efficiently while maintaining the quality of the platform and experience.

Basic Steps to Get Started:

1. **Market Research**: Conduct comprehensive market research to understand the target audience, key competitors, and market trends.

2. **Define the Vision and Mission**: Establish the start-up's ethos, target audience, and main goals, which will guide business and product development directions.

3. **Draft a Business Plan**: Develop a detailed business plan outlining the business model, revenue streams, marketing strategies, and a roadmap for growth.

4. **Assemble a Team**: Attract skilled professionals with relevant experience in technology, wellness and fitness, marketing, and business development.

5. **Develop a Minimum Viable Product (MVP)**: Create, launch, and test an MVP to gauge user feedback, confirm product/market fit, and identify areas for improvement.

6. **Secure Funding**: Seek seed funding from angel investors, venture capital firms, or through crowdfunding platforms.

7. **Marketing and User Acquisition**: Execute targeted marketing and advertising campaigns to build brand awareness and acquire users, focusing on priority demographics.

8. **Continuous Improvement**: Measure performance metrics, analyze feedback, and incorporate user insights to consistently improve features, user experience, and platform functionality.

A community-driven wellness platform start-up business in 2024 would capitalize on the expanding wellness market, an increasingly health-conscious society, and the demand for personalized, holistic wellness experiences. By following the basic steps outlined, the start-up could lay a strong foundation for success in this competitive yet promising space.

JAIME GEHLY

Sustainability and Environment

Sustainable Packaging Solutions

In 2024, a sustainable packaging solutions start-up business would experience tremendous success due to the increased global awareness for environmental sustainability and rapid innovations in eco-friendly packaging materials. Market demand, regulatory changes, and consumer preferences all converge to create a favorable environment for a start-up in this industry.

Key Factors:

1. **Market Growth and Demand**: The push for sustainability has been growing in recent years, and by 2024, it is expected to reach new heights. As more corporations and consumers become increasingly environmentally conscious, there is a high demand for eco-friendly packaging materials. The market for sustainable packaging is on the rise, with a multibillion-dollar global value and an estimated CAGR (Compound Annual Growth Rate) of 5.1% from 2018 to 2024.

2. **Regulatory Environment**: Governments worldwide are implementing stricter regulations in response to environmental concerns. In 2024, businesses are expected to comply with rigorous standards related to the reduction of single-use plastics and lower carbon emissions. A start-up focused on sustainable packaging can capitalize on these policies and position itself as a solution provider for companies looking to adapt and comply with new green mandates.

3. **Consumer Preferences**: Consumer sentiment is shifting rapidly towards a preference for sustainable packaging options. This trend is fueled by educational campaigns, environmental activism, and an increased understanding of the negative impacts of non-biodegradable packaging materials. Due to these factors, companies are more likely to opt for eco-friendly packaging solutions in 2024.

Basic Steps to Get Started:

1. **Market Research**: Identify the industries wanting to transition to eco-friendly packaging, analyze the competition, and evaluate the latest trends and innovative materials in the market. This information will help in developing a strong business plan tailored to your target market.

2. **Business Registration and Legal Compliance**: Register your business and trademark, and choose an appropriate business structure (sole proprietorship, partnership, LLC, or corporation). Ensure you have the necessary permits, licenses, and certifications that adhere to local, national, and international regulations related to the packaging industry.

3. **Sourcing Sustainable Materials**: Identify and source sustainable, eco-friendly materials that cater to your business's target markets. Working with reliable and certified suppliers will help in obtaining high-quality and responsibly-produced materials.

4. **Develop a Portfolio of Products**: Design and develop a diverse range of innovative sustainable packaging products tailored to the needs of your target industries. Focus on functionality, user experience, and aesthetics to ensure that the products are appealing to customers and can compete in the market.

5. **Strategic Partnerships**: Forge strategic partnerships with manufacturers and distributors. Collaborate with companies and organizations committed to sustainable practices, which can lead to valuable networking and business opportunities.

6. **Marketing and Promotion**: Utilize both digital and traditional marketing methods to build your brand's presence and showcase your sustainable ideas. Platforms like social media, content marketing, and industry events are essential to create a buzz around your products and communicate your company's environmental mission.

7. **Continuous Innovation and Improvement**: Stay informed about emerging technologies and innovative sustainable materials. Adapt to industry changes and customer preferences while refining your products and maintaining a competitive edge.

JAIME GEHLY

Renewable Energy Solutions

As the world continues to grapple with climate change and the increasing demand for clean and sustainable energy sources, renewable energy solutions have emerged as a prime topic of interest. By 2024, a Renewable Energy Solutions start-up business will have various opportunities for success in the global market, driven by growing environmental awareness, favorable government policies, and advances in technology.

Key Factors:

Market Demand: The demand for renewable energy has been on the rise in recent years, with wind, solar, and hydropower becoming more relevant and economically viable. This trend is expected to continue as governments and industries push for a global energy transition. The Paris Agreement's goals and the United Nations' Sustainable Development Goals on affordable, reliable, and clean energy contribute to the attractive market conditions in 2024.

Favorable Government Policies: Many governments around the world have committed to ambitious renewable energy targets and are implementing policies to encourage its deployment. Incentives such as tax breaks, grants, and subsidies help level the playing field for renewable energy start-ups, making it easier for them to thrive in competitive markets.

Technological Advancements: By 2024, significant advancements in renewable energy technologies will have made them more efficient, affordable, and effective. Innovations in energy storage, grid integration, and IoT-based energy management systems will allow renewable energy start-ups to offer better solutions to their customers.

Steps to Start a Renewable Energy Solutions Start-up in 2024:

1. **Market Research**: Conduct thorough market research to understand the needs and gaps in the market, identify potential customers, and evaluate the competitive landscape.

2. **Define the Business Model**: Determine the specific services and solutions the start-up will provide, such as solar panel installations, wind turbine maintenance, energy storage systems, or energy consulting services.

3. **Develop a Business Plan**: Create a comprehensive business plan that covers mission and vision statements, target market, competitive analysis, marketing strategy, organizational structure, and financial projections.

4. **Legal Structure and Registration**: Select an appropriate legal structure, such as a sole proprietorship, partnership, or limited liability company (LLC), and register the business with the relevant local, state, and federal authorities.

5. **Acquire Licenses and Permits**: Depending on the location and nature of the start-up, obtain necessary licenses and permits to ensure compliance with regulations and industry standards.

6. **Secure Funding**: Identify potential sources of funding, which can include personal savings, angel investors, venture capital, or government grants and subsidies, and procure the necessary capital to launch the business.

7. **Build a Team**: Recruit skilled professionals, including engineers, technicians, sales and marketing personnel, and project managers, to create a strong and diverse team that will contribute to the start-up's success.

8. **Establish Partnerships**: Collaborate with other companies, industry experts, and associations to develop strategic partnerships for resource sharing, market expansion, or joint ventures.

9. **Marketing and Branding**: Develop a strong brand identity and implement effective marketing strategies, incorporating digital marketing, public relations, trade shows, and industry events, to promote the start-up's services and solutions.

In 2024, a Renewable Energy Solutions start-up will have immense opportunities for success due to increasing demand, favorable policies, and technological advancements. By following the mentioned steps and staying agile in the evolving renewable energy landscape, a start-up can build a flourishing venture and positively contribute to the global energy transition.

Green Transport Methods

As global concerns for climate change, air pollution, and depletion of fossil fuels continue to rise, there is a growing demand for sustainable transport solutions. Green transport methods provide an environmentally friendly alternative to traditional options, offering businesses and individuals cleaner and more energy-efficient modes of transportation. Starting a green transport methods start-up in 2024 provides a timely opportunity to capitalize on this increasing demand while contributing to a more sustainable future.

Why a Green Transport Methods Start-Up Will Be Successful in 2024:

1. **Heightened Environmental Awareness**: The widespread public concern for a cleaner and healthier environment has resulted in governments and private entities looking for greener transport solutions. With global climate commitments and emission targets, a green transport start-up has immense potential to offer environmentally friendly alternatives and succeed in this market.

2. **Technological Advancements**: In 2024, the advancements in green technologies like electric vehicles (EVs), hydrogen fuel cells, and innovative battery systems offer excellent opportunities for introducing new and more efficient transport methods.

3. **Increased Government Support and Incentives**: Governments around the world have started providing incentives, grants, and subsidies to green transport businesses and customers. This financial support creates a conducive environment for green transport method start-ups to thrive.

4. **Consumer Shift Towards Sustainable Choices**: People are increasingly considering the environmental impact of their decisions, and there is a growing preference for eco-friendly transportation options. In a market driven by customer demand, a green transport methods start-up is well-positioned for success.

Basic Steps to Get Started:

1. **Identify a Niche**: Focus on a specific segment of the green transport market that is in demand and underserved. This could be electric bikes, shared electric scooters, ride-sharing platforms, or hydrogen fuel cell vehicles.

2. **Attractive Business Model**: Develop a comprehensive, scalable, and sustainable business model that sets your start-up apart from competitors.

3. **Conduct Market Research**: Gain thorough understanding of the market, customer preferences, and industry trends. Perform a competitive analysis to comprehend what works well and identify gaps that can be exploited by your start-up.

4. **Develop a Business Plan**: Write a detailed business plan that includes mission and vision statements, target market, revenue model, pricing strategy, distribution channels, and marketing plans.

5. **Secure Funding**: Seek out investors, grants, and loans to fund your start-up. Utilize the government incentives and programs available for green transport businesses.

6. **Build a Strong Team**: Recruit a diverse team with the right mix of knowledge and skills in transport, technology, marketing, and sustainability.

7. **Develop Necessary Infrastructure**: Acquire or build the infrastructure needed for your green transport methods, such as charging stations, hydrogen refueling stations, or fleet management software systems.

8. **Legal and Regulatory Compliance**: Obtain necessary licenses, insurance, and permits required to operate a green transport start-up. Also, ensure compliance with local, state, and federal regulations.

9. **Launch a Marketing Campaign**: Create comprehensive marketing strategies to build brand awareness and customer acquisition. Use targeted online and offline channels to reach your audience effectively.

10. **Implement Customer Feedback**: Continuously engage with customers and adapt to their needs to ensure your green transport methods meet their expectations.

In conclusion, the market dynamics in 2024 are favorable for green transport methods start-ups, with environmental awareness, technological advancements, and consumer preferences aligning to create a thriving business environment. By taking the necessary steps to get started, entrepreneurs can capitalize on this opportunity and help shape a cleaner, more sustainable transport industry for the future.

Smart Waste Management Solutions

In 2024, Smart Waste Management Solutions are primed to become a highly successful and profitable start-up domain. As the global population continues to rise, the volume of waste increases accordingly, leading to challenges in waste management. This emerging industry focuses on IoT-based systems and big data analysis to optimize waste collection logistics and improve resource utilization. Entrepreneurs seeking to start a successful business in the waste-management sector must consider a few basic steps to get started.

Market Trends and Growth Drivers:

1. **Increasing Population and Urbanization**: The growth in global population and rapid urbanization lead to a rise in waste generation, intensifying the need for efficient and sustainable waste management solutions. This inescapable need provides a fertile ground for Smart Waste Management Solutions start-ups.

2. **Environmental Awareness and Regulations**: Governments and industries are increasingly focusing on sustainable waste management practices in response to pressing climate change issues. As a result, new policies and regulations incentivize environmentally-friendly waste management techniques, providing a financial advantage to Smart Waste Management Solutions start-ups.

3. **Advances in IoT and Big Data**: The ongoing innovations in IoT and big data technology enable start-ups to provide sophisticated waste management systems that monitor, manage, and analyze waste levels in real-time, reducing operational costs while optimizing resource utilization.

4. **Public-Private Partnerships**: Collaboration between governments and private start-ups can not only fund initial investments but also provide access to essential infrastructure and support services, opening the door for market growth in the Smart Waste Management domain.

5. **Growing Interest from Investors**: Due to the increased focus on sustainability and the expected lucrative returns, investors are drawn to the potential in the Smart Waste Management Solutions sector.

Basic Steps to Get Started:

1. **Research and Understand the Market**: Conduct a thorough market study to identify key trends and unique selling points (USPs) in the waste management sector. Investigate existing competition and assess opportunities for new solutions.

2. **Develop a Technologically Advanced Solution**: Design an innovative solution that leverages IoT, big data, and AI to enable efficient waste collection, monitoring, and analysis. Ensure that your solution complies with environmental regulations.

3. **Identify Target Market and Segment**: Pinpoint your target customer base, be it municipalities, businesses, or residential societies. Determine the best market segments to cater to, considering factors like geolocation, waste type, and volume.

4. **Develop a Business Plan**: Create a comprehensive business plan that outlines your objectives, sales projections, marketing strategies, operational plans, and financial requirements. This will serve as a roadmap and make securing investments or partnerships easier.

5. **Establish Partnerships and Network**: Collaborate with government entities, local municipalities, and waste management stakeholders. Establish relationships with suppliers, IoT technology providers, and investors to ensure a strong foundation for your start-up.

6. **Obtain Necessary Permits and Licenses**: Comply with all legal and regulatory requirements. Acquire the necessary permits, certifications, and licenses needed to operate your Smart Waste Management start-up.

7. **Assemble a Skilled Team**: Hire a team of experts and professionals specialized in waste management, IoT, and big data to execute your project successfully.

8. **Launch and Continuously Improve**: Introduce your Smart Waste Management Solutions to the market and monitor customer feedback. Continually assess your solution's performance and refine it as needed to ensure its long-term success.

The growing need for efficient, environmentally-friendly waste management solutions, combined with advances in technology, positions the Smart Waste Management Solutions start-up sector for immense success and profitability.

JAIME GEHLY

Energy Storage Solutions

As the world transitions towards cleaner, more sustainable energy sources, the demand for energy storage solutions is set to surge. A start-up business focusing on this sector in 2024 will be highly successful and profitable, as governments, communities, businesses, and individuals increasingly invest in greener, more efficient energy systems. This paper outlines key reasons for this success and details the basic steps required to kick-start an energy storage solutions enterprise.

Growing Market Demand:

1. **Global Push for Renewable Energy**: With governments worldwide adopting strong policies to reduce greenhouse gas emissions, support for renewable energy sources such as solar and wind is surging. Since these energy sources are intermittent, efficient energy storage solutions are crucial to ensure a reliable, continuous supply of power.

2. **Adoption of Electric Vehicles (EVs)**: As EVs become more mainstream, the need for advanced energy storage systems—both in vehicles and for charging stations—will grow exponentially.

3. **Grid Modernization**: Aging electrical grids must adapt to accommodate clean energy and evolving consumption patterns. Energy storage solutions enable grid resilience, stability, and increased flexibility.

4. **Reduced Technology Costs**: Technological advancements and economies of scale have led to lower battery costs, making energy storage solutions more economically attractive.

5. **Energy Access and Rural Electrification**: Off-grid and microgrid energy storage systems are significant in providing electricity to remote or underserved regions, contributing to social progress and economic growth.

Starting an Energy Storage Solutions Start-Up:

1. **Market Research**: Conduct thorough market research to identify target customers, evaluate competition, determine which technology and applications to focus on, and assess overall feasibility.

2. **Business Plan**: Create a detailed business plan outlining company objectives, strategies, financial projections, market positioning, and key milestones.

3. **Legal Requirements**: Register the business, obtain necessary licenses and permits, and comply with applicable regulations (e.g., safety standards, waste management).

4. **Assemble a Team**: Hire skilled professionals with experience in engineering, energy system management, business development, and marketing to form a strong team that drives the company's success.

5. **Technology and Innovation**: Identify and invest in the most advanced technologies and applications, and foster an innovation-driven culture to stay ahead of the competition.

6. **Funding**: Secure funding through various channels such as grants, bank loans, angel investors, or venture capital to support initial and ongoing operations and growth.

7. **Product Development**: Design, test, and refine solutions to meet customers' needs and applicable standards while striving for optimal safety, efficiency, and reliability.

8. **Marketing and Sales**: Implement effective marketing strategies to generate awareness about the start-up, its products, and its services. Develop a strong sales pipeline and establish long-term relationships with customers.

9. **Partnerships and Collaborations**: Forge strategic partnerships with renewable energy providers, utility companies, and other market players to foster integration, innovation, and mutual growth.

By seizing the immense opportunities presented by the ever-growing energy storage sector, an energy storage solutions start-up business in 2024 will be well-positioned to thrive and contribute to a greener, more sustainable future.

Circular Economy Marketplaces

In 2024, a circular economy marketplaces start-up business has the potential to become a significant money maker due to the increasing global focus on sustainability, growing consumer demand for environmentally responsible products, and technological advancements that enable efficient business processes. This one-page summary provides an overview of the opportunities presented by circular economy marketplaces, and outlines the basic steps to establish a business in this promising domain.

The circular economy is based on the principles of reducing waste, extending the lifecycle of products, and promoting recycling and reuse. Marketplaces that adhere to these principles have emerged as an innovative business model, addressing the needs of environmentally conscious consumers and contributing to sustainable development. As the concept gains traction, it presents a lucrative opportunity for start-ups focusing on circular economy marketplaces.

Reasons for the Business Potential in 2024:

1. **Growing Awareness and Demand**: The global community is increasingly concerned about climate change and environmental degradation. As a result, consumers are progressively seeking environmentally friendly products and services. This shift in consumer attitudes provides a growing market for circular economy marketplaces, which offer sustainable alternatives to traditional consumption patterns.

2. **Supportive Government Policies**: Governments around the world are enacting legislation and offering incentives to promote the circular economy, such as extended producer responsibility (EPR) regulations, waste management policies, tax breaks, and subsidies. These measures make it easier for start-ups operating within the circular economy to flourish.

3. **Technological Advancements**: The rise of digital platforms, artificial intelligence, internet of things (IoT), and blockchain technology enable efficient and transparent circular economy marketplaces. These technologies facilitate seamless integration of supply chain networks, reduce costs, and minimize inefficiencies for start-ups.

Basic Steps to Get Started:

1. **Market Research and Niche Selection**: Conduct thorough research on current market trends, consumer preferences, and existing competitors to identify gaps and opportunities. Choose a specific niche that aligns with circular economy principles and has growth potential.

2. **Business Plan Development**: Develop a comprehensive business plan that outlines your value proposition, target market, revenue model, and the technological infrastructure needed to support your marketplace start-up. Address the financial, logistical, and legal aspects of the business, and include a strategic roadmap for growth.

3. **Building the Platform**: Design and develop a user-friendly digital platform that simplifies transactions, allows seamless communication between buyers and sellers, and integrates necessary features such as reviews, product tracking, and secure payment gateways. Utilize cutting-edge technologies like AI and blockchain for efficient supply chain management, inventory tracking, and fraud prevention.

4. **Marketing and Branding**: Establish a strong brand identity that reflects your commitment to sustainability and target audience preferences. Develop a marketing strategy encompassing social media, content marketing, and influencer partnerships to create awareness about your marketplace and generate interest.

5. **Network Development**: Forge partnerships with relevant producers, designers, and manufacturers who prioritize circular economy principles. Collaborate with waste management facilities, recycling centers, and refurbishing service providers to ensure the availability of sustainable products and services on your platform.

6. **Launch and Scale**: Soft-launch your marketplace platform to a select audience for feedback and iterative improvements. Gradually expand your services to a broader market, scale your operations, and explore opportunities for geographic or product-based expansion.

In conclusion, 2024 presents a unique opportunity for start-ups to enter the circular economy marketplace, leveraging growing consumer demand and supportive regulatory frameworks.

JAIME GEHLY

Carbon Capture and Storage Solutions

In 2024, the race to solve climate change issues has reached an unprecedented level, with governments, industries, and individuals around the world acknowledging the urgent need to reduce CO_2 emissions. One of the key solutions to this problem, Carbon Capture and Storage (CCS), has gained significant attention due to its potential to sequester and store vast amounts of carbon dioxide from various emission sources. This, in turn, has created an incredible market opportunity for startups focusing on CCS solutions.

1. **Market Demand**: As governments and corporates set ambitious carbon reduction targets, the market demand for CCS technology has increased exponentially. Industries such as power generation, cement, steel, and petrochemicals are actively seeking effective ways to reduce their carbon footprint. Moreover, NGOs and environmental organizations are pressuring companies to adopt CCS, while investors and consumers alike demand sustainable practices. This market pressure makes CCS solutions an attractive business opportunity in 2024.

2. **Regulatory Incentives**: Climate policies have encouraged the adoption of CCS technology. Governments worldwide have implemented carbon pricing and incentive schemes, such as tax credits and subsidies, to promote the adoption of CCS technology. These policies make it financially appealing for companies to invest in CCS projects and provide a fertile environment for startups to grow.

3. **Technological Innovation**: Rapid advancements in technology have made CCS solutions more efficient and cost-effective than ever before. From Direct Air Capture to Enhanced Oil Recovery (EOR), startup businesses have a plethora of innovative technologies at their disposal. As a result, the potential return on investment has skyrocketed, making it more attractive for investors to fund CCS startups.

4. **Global Collaboration**: Climate change mitigation requires global solutions. With increasing awareness, collaborative efforts between governments, research institutions, and private entities are on the rise to develop and deploy advanced CCS methods. This collaborative environment provides an excellent platform for startup businesses to thrive and profit from a wide range of partnerships and resources.

To Get Started with a CCS Start-Up Business, Consider the Following:

1. **Identify Your Niche**: Define what specific CCS solution your company will focus on – be it Direct Air Capture, Carbon Mineralization, or CCS use in specific industries. Conduct thorough market research to assess existing players, demand, and opportunities to stand out.

2. **Develop a Business Plan**: Craft a comprehensive business plan that includes an overview of your startup, industry analysis, market research, and financial projections. This will help structure your activities and attract investors.

3. **Secure Funding**: Identify potential funding sources such as angel investors, venture capital, seed funding, or government grants that fit your business needs. Prepare a solid pitch to showcase your idea, team, and roadmap to success.

4. **Assemble a Qualified Team**: Build a team composed of knowledgeable professionals from diverse backgrounds, such as science, engineering, finance, and marketing. Such a team will ensure successful R&D, financial management, and market outreach.

5. **Establish Partnerships**: Partner with established firms or research institutions to leverage complementary capabilities, experience, and resources for mutual growth.

6. **Regulatory Compliance**: Ensure that your startup adheres to the necessary laws, regulations, and environmental standards, both locally and globally.

In conclusion, a Carbon Capture and Storage solutions startup presents a promising opportunity for entrepreneurs in 2024. With an increasing market demand, regulatory incentives, innovative technologies, and global collaboration, now is the right time to launch a lucrative business in one of the most critical areas of sustainability.

Sustainable Event Planning

In 2024, a sustainable event planning start-up business is a smart and successful choice, as the global market witnesses an increased emphasis on responsible consumption and environmental stewardship. By embracing green initiatives, this start-up will cater to the growing demand for eco-friendly events, provide a competitive edge, and create a positive impact on the environment.

Rationale:

1. **Growing Demand for Sustainable Events**: As awareness of ecological issues such as climate change and resource depletion expands, more businesses and individuals are opting for greener alternatives. Companies increasingly prefer to be associated with environmentally responsible events to improve their corporate image and meet stakeholder expectations.

2. **Market Differentiation**: By adopting sustainable practices, a start-up event planning company will differentiate itself from competitors and position the business as a forward-thinking, environmentally responsible choice for clients.

3. **Regulations and Incentives**: Government bodies and industry associations are increasingly implementing sustainability-related regulations and guidelines for events. Consequently, it will be crucial for businesses to stay ahead of the curve by adopting eco-friendly practices. Furthermore, there are financial incentives and potential cost savings when adopting sustainable measures.

Basic Steps to Start the Sustainable Event Planning Business:

1. **Develop the Business Concept**: Clearly define the vision, mission, and purpose of the sustainable event planning start-up. Describe the range of services offered and determine the business structure (sole proprietorship, LLC, partnership, etc.).

2. **Conduct Market Research**: Study the market to understand the demand for sustainable event planning services, identify target clients, and analyze competitors' offerings. This study will be crucial in refining the business concept and identifying growth opportunities.

3. **Create a Business Plan**: Develop a comprehensive business plan encompassing marketing strategy, financial projections, and operational details.

The plan should also include the company's sustainability goals and measures to achieve them.

4. **Register and License the Business**: Follow local and national regulations to register the business, obtain required licenses, and handle any tax implications.

5. **Establish a Brand Identity**: Design a strong brand identity featuring the company's sustainable values. This includes creating a logo, business cards, promotional materials, and an engaging website.

6. **Develop a Network**: Establish a wide network within the events sphere, including suppliers, venues, and local businesses. Work towards forging strong relationships with eco-friendly and ethical providers to deliver sustainable events effectively.

7. **Acquire Relevant Certifications**: Pursue sustainability-related certifications, such as the LEED (Leadership in Energy and Environmental Design) or ISO 20121, to enhance credibility and demonstrate commitment to eco-friendly practices.

8. **Implement Sustainable Event Practices**: Emphasize waste management, resource conservation, energy efficiency, and sustainable procurement within event planning and production.

9. **Market the Start-Up**: Utilize digital marketing and social media platforms to showcase the unique value proposition, client experiences, and in-depth case studies highlighting environmental impacts and successes.

In conclusion, launching a sustainable event planning start-up in 2024 is a prudent and rewarding decision, given the increase in eco-conscious demand and growing focus on environmental well-being. By focusing on sustainability, such a start-up stands to gain a competitive advantage, capitalize on market opportunities, and contribute positively to the environment.

Carbon Offset Marketplace

With increasing awareness of climate change and rising demand for sustainable solutions, a carbon offset marketplace start-up is an excellent business opportunity in 2024. Such an initiative allows organizations and individuals to purchase carbon credits to offset their own emissions, supporting global efforts to combat climate change. This one-page summary outlines the potential of a carbon offset marketplace start-up and details the basic steps required for launching it successfully.

Market Opportunity:

In recent years, organizations and individuals have become more committed to reducing their carbon footprint. The Paris Agreement and other international measures to combat climate change have urged companies to take responsibility for their emissions. As a result, the demand for carbon offset solutions is expected to grow tremendously.

Furthermore, start-ups can play a crucial role in generating innovative, technology-driven solutions in the carbon offset market. The need to track, verify, and report on various carbon credit projects presents sizeable market potential, and governments across the globe are increasingly investing in sustainable energy initiatives.

Steps to Launch a Carbon Offset Marketplace Start-Up:

1. **Market Research**: Thoroughly research the carbon offset industry, potential customers, competitors, and existing solutions. Assess strengths and weaknesses, and identify market gaps that can be addressed by your start-up.

2. **Develop a Business Model**: Design a sustainable and scalable business model that targets organizations and individuals looking for carbon offset solutions. Consider the type of clients your business will serve, the scale, and the specific niches of interest.

3. **Regulatory Compliance**: Obtain necessary licenses and ensure compliance with relevant national and international regulations. Stay up-to-date with environmental laws, carbon credit trading rules, and transparency requirements.

4. **Source Carbon Credits**: Partner with certified carbon credit projects to curate and offer a range of high-quality, verified carbon offsets. Look for projects with

high environmental and social impact, like reforestation, renewable energy, and energy efficiency initiatives.

5. **Develop a Platform**: Create an intuitive, user-friendly online platform where users can easily search, compare, and purchase carbon offsets. Implement robust tracking and analytics capabilities to ensure transparency and verify the impact of purchased offsets.

6. **Marketing and Promotion**: Develop a comprehensive marketing strategy to effectively promote your carbon offset marketplace. Employ digital marketing channels like social media, content marketing, and search engine optimization (SEO) to increase awareness and attract potential customers.

7. **Partnerships and Networking**: Collaborate with industry players, environmental NGOs, and other relevant stakeholders to expand your network and gain credibility. Promote your start-up at industry events, global conferences, and sustainability workshops.

8. **Customer Support and Education**: Provide excellent customer support and educational resources to help clients understand the importance of carbon offsets and the impact of their purchases. Offer detailed guidelines and frequently asked questions (FAQs) on your platform.

Given the heightened urgency to tackle climate change, a carbon offset marketplace start-up presents an attractive business opportunity in 2024. By following the steps outlined above, this venture can provide an effective solution for organizations and individuals seeking to minimize their environmental impact and contribute to global sustainability.

Sustainable Fashion Resale Platforms

A sustainable fashion resale platform start-up business has immense potential in 2024 due to the growing concerns about climate change, increasing demand for eco-friendly products, and the positive shift towards circular economy models. This platform will not only benefit the environment but also present lucrative opportunities for entrepreneurs.

Why Sustainable Fashion Resale Platform is a Good Business:

1. **Addressing Climate Change**: As climate change continues to be a dominant global issue, awareness about sustainable living increases. This business idea capitalizes on the growing interest in reducing carbon footprint, textile waste, and curbing over-consumption.

2. **Growing Market**: The resale market has been growing rapidly, showcasing the widespread interest in sustainable solutions. By tapping into this ever-expanding market, entrepreneurs can anticipate steady profits and increased value over time.

3. **Affordable and Stylish Options**: The platform allows users to access a variety of stylish, eco-friendly clothing at affordable prices. This appeals to cost-conscious and environmentally-minded customers, further solidifying the platform's staying power in the marketplace.

4. **Circular Economy**: This business supports the circular economy by encouraging reuse, recycling, and upcycling, substantially reducing waste in the apparel industry.

5. **Job Opportunities**: A sustainable fashion resale platform can generate a variety of job opportunities, from tech-based roles to logistics, marketing, and customer support.

Basic Steps to Get Started:

1. **Market Research**: Conduct comprehensive market research to identify target demographics, their buying habits, and preferences to define your value proposition.

2. **Competitor Analysis**: Assess and analyze existing competitors to understand what works, what doesn't, and how you can differentiate from them.

3. **Business Model**: Design your business model, including how the platform will operate, pricing strategy, sourcing inventory, and revenue streams such as consignment or buy-sell-trade models.

4. **Technology Development**: Develop or procure a user-friendly website or app with features like detailed product listings, search filters, payment integrations, and social media sharing options.

5. **Inventory Management**: Determine how to source and manage inventory. Establish partnerships with suppliers, brands, or individuals for the provision of quality, sustainable garments.

6. **Marketing and Branding**: Develop a strong brand identity and marketing strategy. Utilize social media, content marketing, partnerships, and influencers to raise awareness about your platform and its mission.

7. **Legal and Finance**: Register your business, seek necessary permits, and acquire insurance coverage. Establish an accounting system and, if needed, secure funding through investors or alternative financing options.

8. **Logistics**: Set up an efficient shipping system and create a clear returns policy. Determine warehousing and storage facilities if necessary.

9. **Customer Service**: Develop a customer support system to address inquiries, resolution of issues, and foster a loyal customer base.

A sustainable fashion resale platform start-up can not only offer a cost-effective and environmentally friendly alternative to fast fashion but also create significant opportunities for growth and revenue generation in 2024. By following these essential steps, entrepreneurs can capitalize on the shifting market demands and contribute to a greener future.

JAIME GEHLY

Hydroponic Home Garden Systems

Hydroponic home garden systems have recently emerged as a highly promising and potentially lucrative business venture for 2024. These systems provide individuals with an innovative method of growing plants in nutrient-rich water, without soil. By capitalizing on burgeoning trends in sustainability and self-sufficiency, as well as offering numerous benefits to both consumers and the environment, hydroponic home garden systems are well-positioned for success in the modern marketplace.

Key Points:

1. **Growing Market Demand**: In 2024, the world will continue to grapple with numerous environmental, societal, and health concerns. As a result, more people will actively seek sustainable and healthy food options, contributing to a surge in demand for urban farming solutions, such as hydroponic home garden systems.

2. **Environmental Benefits**: Hydroponic systems have a considerably lower environmental impact compared to traditional agriculture due to reduced water consumption, waste production, and land-use requirements. With global attention increasingly focused on climate change and sustainable living, eco-friendly initiatives such as hydroponic systems will garner considerable interest and support.

3. **Versatility and High Crop Yields**: Hydroponic home garden systems can accommodate a variety of plant species, enabling users to grow diverse produce throughout the year. Additionally, these systems offer an optimal growing environment, ensuring consistently high crop yields regardless of external conditions.

4. **Health Benefits**: A growing interest in wellness and avoiding pesticide residues on fruits and vegetables will bolster the hydroponic home garden systems' appeal. By providing consumers with access to organic produce, hydroponic gardening represents an attractive alternative to conventional produce.

Basic Steps to Start a Hydroponic Home Garden Systems Business:

1. **Market Research**: Conduct a thorough analysis of the market, its current state, and potential growth opportunities. Be sure to study your competition, and learn from their successes and failures. Consider various business models, target audiences, and pricing structures.

2. **Business Plan**: Develop a detailed business plan outlining your company's mission, vision, and objectives. This plan should cover financial projections, marketing strategies, and operational details. Additionally, establish the necessary structure (corporation, LLC, etc.) for your business.

3. **Product Selection and Development**: Determine the types of hydroponic systems you will offer, including their specifications, sizes, and additional features. Research available technology and suppliers for components, and develop systems that cater to your target market and stand out from competitors.

4. **Licensing and Permits**: Obtain the necessary permits and licenses required for starting a hydroponic gardening business within your target area. This may include, but is not limited to, certifications from health departments, agricultural boards, and your local municipality.

5. **Establish Your Supply Chain**: Develop relationships with suppliers and manufacturers to ensure you have access to quality components, materials, and resources. This step is crucial for maintaining a consistent, reliable inventory.

6. **Marketing and Sales Strategy**: Create an effective marketing strategy that promotes your unique selling points and raises brand awareness. Focus on promoting the environmental, health, and versatility benefits of hydroponic home garden systems. Utilize both digital and traditional marketing channels for a comprehensive approach.

7. **Set up and Launch**: Once everything is in place, establish your physical and/or online presence, set up your inventory and logistics, and officially launch your business.

As environmental concerns and the demand for sustainable living continue to grow, hydroponic home garden systems present an attractive business opportunity for 2024. With the right strategy and commitment, this start-up venture promises significant profits, customer satisfaction, and environmental benefits.

JAIME GEHLY

Smart City Infrastructure Solutions

In recent years, smart city technologies have emerged as a major force in the quest to improve urban living conditions, streamline municipal services, and optimize city management. By 2024, the implementation of smart city initiatives has become a necessity rather than a luxury for cities around the world. A start-up business focusing on smart city infrastructure solutions presents a timely and lucrative opportunity. This report highlights the reasons behind the increasing demand for smart city infrastructure solutions and outlines the basic steps required to establish a startup venture in this sector.

Key Factors:

1. **Rising Global Urbanization**: As urban populations continue to grow rapidly, cities face immense challenges in providing essential services such as transportation, housing, and utilities. A smart city infrastructure solutions start-up is poised to benefit from this global trend, offering technological innovations that make cities more efficient, sustainable, and resident-friendly.

2. **Government Support and Policies**: By 2024, an increasing number of governments worldwide have recognized the importance of transitioning to smart cities. Various grants, tax incentives, and subsidies are provided to encourage the development, deployment, and adoption of smart city technologies. This further boosts the potential for a start-up in the sector.

3. **Environment and Sustainability**: Climate change, environmental pollution, and resource depletion have intensified the need for cities to develop and integrate green technologies. A smart city infrastructure solutions start-up can provide eco-friendly solutions in areas such as energy efficiency, waste management, and water conservation.

4. **Public-Private Partnerships**: With significant investments being made by governments and private entities, there is an increasing demand for public-private partnerships to drive the development and implementation of smart city technologies. A start-up specializing in smart city infrastructure solutions can capitalize on these opportunities.

To launch a Successful Smart City Infrastructure Solutions Start-Up in 2024, the Following Basic Steps are Recommended:

1. **Identify a Niche**: To stand out in a competitive market, start by identifying a specific niche within the smart city ecosystem where the business can excel. This could include areas such as smart grid technology, intelligent transportation systems, or innovative waste management solutions.

2. **Develop a Comprehensive Business Plan**: A well-constructed business plan contains a detailed overview of the company vision, target markets, products and services offerings, competitive analysis, financial projections, and marketing strategy.

3. **Secure Funding**: Given the significant appetite for green technology and the governmental support for smart cities, there are numerous funding opportunities available. These include venture capital, angel investors, grants, and government incentives. Take advantage of these opportunities to secure the required financing for the start-up.

4. **Assemble a Skilled Team**: The success of any start-up largely depends on its team's expertise and passion. Assemble a team of professionals with diverse backgrounds, including IT, engineering, urban planning, marketing, and business operations, to ensure that the company has the right blend of skills and experience.

5. **Foster Partnerships**: Collaborate with key stakeholders such as technology vendors, universities, and other businesses within the smart city ecosystem to leverage complementary expertise and resources. Establishing strong partnerships will help the start-up tap into diverse opportunities and scale up its operations faster.

In conclusion, a smart city infrastructure solutions start-up constitutes a highly promising business prospect in 2024, given the rapid global urbanization, supportive government policies, heightened environmental concerns, technological advancements, and a strong demand for innovative solutions to complex urban challenges. By taking the necessary steps to establish and grow such a business, entrepreneurs can contribute significantly to transforming urban landscapes and improving the overall quality of life for city dwellers worldwide.

JAIME GEHLY

Peer-To-Peer Electricity Grid

In recent years, there has been a growing global focus on clean energy, decentralized power generation, and energy democratization. As priorities shift toward sustainable development, starting a peer-to-peer (P2P) electricity grid business in 2024 is poised to be a promising venture. This innovative business model addresses environmental and social concerns while capitalizing on significant market opportunities. Below, we will outline the advantages of P2P electricity grids and the essential steps needed to establish a start-up in this sector.

Why a P2P Electricity Grid Start-up Business is a Good Opportunity in 2024:

1. **Decentralized Power Generation**: As societies aim for a greener future, the adoption of decentralized power generation technologies such as solar panels and wind turbines has accelerated. A P2P electricity grid enables individuals and businesses to generate, store, and share their excess renewable energy, creating a stable and self-sufficient power network.

2. **Cost-Efficiency and Energy Savings**: P2P electricity grids empower consumers by allowing them to sell their excess energy at competitive rates. This marketplace mechanism results in lower energy costs for both energy producers and consumers, driving further adoption and fostering economic growth.

3. **Climate Change and Government Incentives**: Governments worldwide are establishing policies and incentives to transition toward renewable energy. Initiating a start-up focusing on P2P electricity grids aligns with these goals and can benefit from various grants, tax breaks, or regulatory support.

4. **Technological Advancements**: The Internet of Things (IoT) and blockchain technology facilitate secure and efficient P2P energy transactions. The development of energy storage solutions and smart grids create a strong foundation for P2P energy trading systems.

Steps to Get Started with a P2P Electricity Grid Start-Up Business:

1. **Market Research**: Begin by conducting comprehensive market research to understand the specific needs and trends within the energy sector, as well as potential competitors and consumer preferences.

2. **Develop Your Business Model**: Next, devise a detailed business plan that outlines your P2P platform's value proposition, target market, revenue streams, and operational model. Additionally, assess any potential partnerships with local utilities or energy companies.

3. **Establish a Legal Entity**: Consult with an attorney specializing in energy law to establish an appropriate legal structure for your business, ensuring compliance with regional and federal regulations.

4. **Obtain Licenses and Permits**: Acquire any necessary permits and licenses needed to operate a P2P electricity grid start-up. These requirements may include grid connection permits, energy trading licenses, and environmental clearances.

5. **Create the P2P Platform**: Develop a secure and user-friendly P2P platform which leverages IoT and blockchain technology to enable efficient energy transactions. Collaborate with technology partners, if necessary.

6. **Network Infrastructure and Installations**: Partner with industry experts and contractors to design and install necessary infrastructure, such as smart meters, energy management systems, and energy storage solutions, to support P2P electricity trading.

7. **Marketing and Customer Acquisition**: Implement targeted marketing strategies to attract both energy producers and consumers to your platform. Collaboration with local communities, awareness campaigns, and partnerships with sustainable development initiatives can contribute to customer acquisition and brand credibility.

8. **Monitor and Optimize**: Continuously monitor your P2P platform's performance and market trends. Adapt your business strategy and make necessary improvements to stay ahead of competitors and maintain long-term success.

In conclusion, a P2P electricity grid start-up business in 2024 leverages the increasing global demand for clean, decentralized energy solutions while empowering individuals and communities. This innovative business model, combined with the necessary steps to establish a successful company, offers a lucrative and responsible venture for forward-thinking entrepreneurs.

JAIME GEHLY

Smart Water Management Systems

With growing awareness about environmental conservation, increasing necessity to optimize resources, and rising emphasis on efficient utility management, Smart Water Management Systems (SWMS) have become integral to modern societies. By 2024, a SWMS start-up will present an excellent opportunity for investment for the following reasons:

Key Factors:

1. **Accelerated Global Demand**: The ongoing water crisis and increasing water scarcity worldwide have created a pressing demand for sustainable water management. Governments, industries, and residential consumers are seeking smart water solutions for efficient management and conservation of this valuable resource, providing ample market growth prospects.

2. **Technological Innovation**: Technological advancements in areas like IoT, machine learning, and AI have paved the way for innovative SWMS. These systems can provide real-time monitoring, leak detection, and predictive analytics, facilitating optimal usage and reducing water wastage.

3. **Supportive Regulations and Policies**: With growing concerns about water security and sustainability, governments worldwide are formulating policies and regulations to alleviate water scarcity. These initiatives will encourage the mass adoption of SWMS, providing significant market opportunities for start-ups.

To Successfully Launch a SWMS Start-Up in 2024, Investors Can Follow These Basic Steps:

1. **Market Research and Feasibility Study**: Perform thorough market research and identify target segments like municipalities, industries, and residential communities. Analyze local and global competition, evaluate water management needs and trends, and assess the feasibility of establishing a SWMS start-up in the target region.

2. **Business Plan Development**: Develop a comprehensive business plan to outline the start-up's goals, target market, revenue sources, costs, and projected profits. This plan should include information on technology/platform selection, product/services portfolio, and a go-to-market strategy.

3. **Legal Structure and Business Registration**: Determine the most fitting legal entity structure for the start-up, considering factors like liability protection, taxation, and regulatory requirements. Register the business with the relevant authorities and obtain necessary licenses and permits.

4. **Financial Planning and Funding**: Prepare a detailed financial plan and decide on the funding sources. Seek angel investors, venture capitalists, or government grants, or consider applying for bank loans. Ensure realistic financial projections to maintain start-up viability.

5. **Technology Development and Partnerships**: Develop proprietary technologies for the SWMS portfolio or form partnerships with established technology providers. Incorporate IoT-enabled devices like smart meters, sensors, cloud computing, and data analytics platforms to create comprehensive SWMS solutions.

6. **Marketing and Promotion**: Create marketing materials and strategies highlighting the value proposition of the SWMS offerings. Focus on understandings unique customer needs and delivering personalized solutions, which will foster stronger relationships and customer retention.

7. **Continuous Improvement**: As the start-up grows and the market landscape evolves, continuously innovate to develop cutting-edge solutions, explore new revenue streams, and expand into untapped markets.

With growing awareness about water conservation and the increasing global demand for efficient resource management, a Smart Water Management System start-up holds significant potential in 2024. By following these basic steps, investors can gain a footing in this booming market and contribute towards the global push for sustainable water management.

JAIME GEHLY

Vertical Aeroponic Farming

The rising global population, decreasing agricultural land, and the increased challenges associated with conventional farming methods have catalyzed the urgency to find alternatives in meeting the world's increasing food demand. In 2024, Vertical Aeroponic Farming (VAF) offers an innovative and viable solution with enormous potential for success in the agriculture industry due to its numerous advantages and strong alignment with sustainability drives worldwide. This report outlines the reasons why a VAF startup would thrive in 2024 and the basic steps required to get started.

Reasons for Success:

1. **Increased Crop Yield**: VAF employs a soil-less and optimized growing environment, resulting in a considerably higher yield than traditional agriculture. Vertical stacking of planters capitalizes on the vertical space available, allowing for more plants per square foot.

2. **Resource Efficiency**: By using a closed-loop circulation system that sprays a nutrient-rich solution, VAF uses up to 95% less water than traditional farming methods. This feature makes it attractive in arid regions and areas where water is scarce.

3. **Reduced Pesticide Use**: The controlled environment in aeroponic farming lowers the risk of pest infestations, considerably reducing the need for chemical pesticides. Consequently, the produce tends to be cleaner, healthier, and more eco-friendly.

4. **Year-Round Production**: VAF's climate-controlled conditions offer consistent production all year round, regardless of external factors such as weather, allowing for a stable supply to the market and addressing issues of seasonal crop variations.

5. **Urban Adaptability**: VAF is location-independent, making it easier to set up operations in urban areas, bringing fresh produce closer to consumers, reducing transportation costs, and decreasing the carbon footprint.

6. **Scalability**: VAF systems are designed to be modular and appealing to investors. Their expandable architecture enables them to be easily scaled to meet the requirements of different-sized operations while maintaining control over the quality of production.

Basic Steps to Start a VAF Startup:

1. **Feasibility Study**: Conduct a feasibility study to understand the market demand, analyze location, and evaluate the overall cost and revenue potential of the VAF system.

2. **Business Planning**: Develop a robust business plan that highlights the operational model, financial projections, marketing strategy, and risk management strategy.

3. **Acquire Funding**: Identify potential funding sources, such as equity investment, loans, grants, and crowdfunding opportunities in the market.

4. **Procuring Equipment and Technology**: Collaborate with leading VAF system providers and technology partners to obtain the required equipment and tools for setting up an advanced VAF facility.

5. **Location Selection**: Determine the optimal location(s) for the startup based on factors such as proximity to consumers and resources, available space in urban centers, and climate requirements.

6. **Legal and Regulatory Compliance**: Complete all paperwork for business registration, licenses, and permits as per local and federal regulations to ensure compliance with agriculture, environmental, and safety standards.

7. **Workforce and Management**: Hire trained personnel for different aspects of the operation, such as horticulturists, technicians, and sales specialists. Implement a well-rounded management system to oversee various aspects of the business.

In conclusion, the increased global emphasis on sustainability, urbanization trends, and resource challenges make Vertical Aeroponic Farming a promising startup opportunity for entrepreneurs looking to make an impact in the Agritech space. By following the basic steps outlined, businesses can capitalize on the numerous advantages VAF offers and position themselves for success in 2024 and beyond.

JAIME GEHLY

Sustainable Product Innovations

In recent years, the focus on sustainability and environmental consciousness has surged, leading to increased demand for green products and eco-friendly solutions. A sustainable product innovations start-up business has immense potential for success in 2024, as consumers and businesses alike recognize the importance of adopting sustainable practices. By providing innovative and eco-friendly products, the start-up can tap into a rapidly growing market driven by increased awareness, shifting consumer preferences, and supportive government regulations. To set the stage for success, the start-up must follow a series of essential steps, from market research to securing funding.

1. **Rising Demand for Sustainable Solutions**: As the world grapples with climate change, resource depletion, and waste management issues, demand for sustainable products and services continues to grow at a rapid pace. This trend presents a market ripe with opportunities for sustainable product innovations, as both consumers and corporations exhibit an enhanced interest in environmentally friendly alternatives.

2. **Shift in Consumer Preferences**: Shifting preferences among consumers towards more sustainable and eco-friendly products have the potential to reshape entire industries. Aligning the start-up's mission with these evolving expectations will help the business attract and retain customers while promoting social responsibility and environmental stewardship.

3. **Government Regulations and Support**: Government policies and regulations promoting sustainability create favorable conditions for such start-ups. These include tax incentives, grants, subsidies, and regulatory frameworks that encourage the development and adoption of sustainable solutions, providing a strategic advantage for innovative start-ups.

4. **Competitive Differentiation**: An increasing number of businesses competing on sustainability offers an opportunity for start-ups to differentiate themselves by providing innovative and unique products that stand out amongst the competition. By focusing on continuous improvement and evolution, the start-up can consistently stay ahead of emerging trends and demands.

To Get Started with the Sustainable Product Innovations Start-Up, Follow These Basic Steps:

1. **Market Research**: Conduct thorough market research to identify untapped opportunities, evaluate current sustainable solutions, and understand the needs and preferences of the target audience. This will allow the start-up to identify gaps in the market and develop innovative products that cater to those needs.

2. **Develop a Business Plan**: Outline the objectives, strategies, and business structure in a comprehensive business plan. Include market analysis, product offerings, marketing strategies, financial projections, and a roadmap for short-term and long-term growth.

3. **Establish an R&D Team**: Assemble a proficient research and development team with diverse skill sets and backgrounds, including experts in environmental science, engineering, design, and marketing. This team will work together to develop innovative and sustainable products that solve real-world problems.

4. **Secure Funding**: Seek out investors or financial institutions that understand the value and importance of sustainable business practices. Develop a compelling pitch highlighting potential market growth, competitive advantages, and the start-up's commitment to creating a positive environmental impact.

5. **Build Partnerships**: Form strategic partnerships with suppliers, manufacturers, and distribution channels to facilitate the production and distribution of the start-up's sustainable products. Collaborate with like-minded businesses, NGOs, and industry influencers to share resources, knowledge, and amplify the start-up's reach.

6. **Marketing and Launch**: Implement an effective marketing campaign that showcases the start-up's unique value proposition, emphasizing the environmental benefits of its products. Utilize a mix of digital marketing techniques, public relations, and grassroots initiatives to engage consumers and create brand awareness. Launch the product line and continuously refine offerings based on customer feedback and evolving market trends.

In conclusion, by addressing the growing demand for sustainable solutions, a sustainable product innovations start-up has the potential to thrive in 2024. By following the outlined steps and remaining adaptive and resilient, this start-up can create a solid foundation for success in the competitive market landscape.

Zero-Waste Product Stores

Rising environmental concerns and evolving consumer awareness have shaped a shining future for zero-waste product stores in 2024. More people are driven to make eco-conscious decisions, pushing businesses to cater to the demand for environmentally friendly, sustainable products. This market shift presents a profitable opportunity for a startup targeting this niche using a zero-waste model, which aims to eliminate waste and promote reusable, recyclable, or biodegradable products.

Reasons for Success:

1. **Growing Environmental Awareness**: The current trajectory towards increased climate change scares presents a unique opportunity for zero-waste business models. People are changing their consumption habits due to increased awareness of environmental issues, making zero-waste stores appealing on a broader scale.

2. **Shift in Consumer Preferences**: Consumers are becoming more concerned about the environmental impact of their purchases, opting for green products and sustainable practices. This shift will drive demand for zero-waste stores, creating a thriving marketplace for eco-friendly goods.

3. **Supportive Regulations and Policies**: Government policies promoting sustainability and waste reduction encourage businesses to adopt eco-friendly practices. Incentives such as tax breaks, rebates, and subsidies targeting zero-waste initiatives create a favorable environment for a start-up in this industry by mitigating risks and investment costs.

4. **Competitive Differentiation**: Zero-waste stores stand out in the market, providing a unique selling proposition with their emphasis on waste reduction. This positioning creates a brand association with environmental responsibility, capturing an increasingly conscientious consumer base seeking to support eco-friendly businesses.

Basic Steps Required to Get Started:

1. **Market Research**: Begin with a thorough market analysis to understand demand, competition, and target consumers. Identify potential gaps and opportunities to build a competitive and successful zero-waste store.

2. **Business Plan & Legal Structure**: Develop a detailed business plan that addresses monetary requirements, location, products and services, marketing strategies, and operational plans. Set up a legal structure with the necessary licenses, permits, and insurance to adhere to regional and industry-specific regulations.

3. **Building a Green Supply Chain**: Source products from responsible, eco-friendly suppliers that adhere to sustainability and fair-trade practices. Carefully curate these products, ensuring they fall within the zero-waste ethos—reusable, recyclable, biodegradable, or compostable.

4. **Store Location & Design**: Choose a visible and accessible location to establish a strong presence. Give attention to sustainable design principles in the store layout, such as energy-efficient lighting, recycled materials, and functional displays that promote zero-waste practices.

5. **Branding & Marketing**: Establish a strong brand identity coherent with the zero-waste mission, emphasizing a commitment to the environment. Develop multi-channel marketing strategies that include social media, PR, events, and collaborations with other eco-friendly organizations to reach and educate target audiences.

6. **Employee Training**: Train employees to support and promote the zero-waste initiatives in-store. Knowledgeable and passionate staff will improve customer experiences and foster loyalty to the brand.

A zero-waste product store startup will be successful in 2024 due to the accelerating transition towards sustainable lifestyles and eco-conscious consumption patterns. By thoughtfully curating products, establishing a strong brand, and providing a unique customer experience, this business model will capitalize on market trends delivering profit and simultaneously contributing to a more sustainable future.

JAIME GEHLY

Native Plant Landscaping Services

With the increasing awareness about environmental sustainability and the benefits of local flora, a native plant landscaping services start-up business has the potential to succeed in 2024. The ecological benefits and cost-effectiveness of native plants have driven the landscaping industry to adopt greener solutions. A well-executed native plant landscaping business can cater to the growing market while also promoting biodiversity, water conservation, and ecological stability.

Reasons for Success:

1. **Growing Ecological Awareness**: Climate change and the worldwide call for sustainable living have led to increased interest in eco-friendly landscaping practices. By focusing on native plants, this start-up caters to the needs of environmentally-conscious consumers.

2. **Biodiversity Preservation**: Native plant landscaping promotes the preservation of local habitats and ecosystems, as it uses plants adapted to the region's specific conditions. This ensures a harmonious and symbiotic relationship between the built and natural environments.

3. **Water Conservation**: The use of native plant species in landscaping reduces the consumption of valuable water resources, as these plants require minimal irrigation compared to non-native plants.

4. **Cost-Effectiveness**: Native plants tend to be more low-maintenance and disease-resistant, leading to lower expenses for homeowners and businesses seeking landscaping services.

5. **Government Incentives**: There has been an increase in federal and state programs that encourage the use of native plant landscaping. These incentives and rebates can be a significant motivation for clients when choosing a landscaping business.

Basic Steps to Get Started:

1. **Market Research**: Conduct thorough market research to identify target demographics, competitors, and potential growth opportunities in the native plant landscaping industry.

2. **Business Plan**: Develop a comprehensive business plan that includes financial projections, marketing strategies, and operational details, such as staffing and equipment requirements.

3. **Legal Framework**: Establish a proper legal structure for the business, taking into account the various permits and licenses needed for landscaping services in your specific location.

4. **Supplier Relationships**: Build relationships with native plant nurseries and suppliers to ensure access to high-quality plants and materials, as well as opportunities for volume discounts and negotiated pricing.

5. **Build a Team**: Recruit experienced and knowledgeable staff with expertise in native plant landscaping, ecology, horticulture, or related fields.

6. **Marketing & Promotion**: Develop a strong marketing strategy that showcases the ecological benefits and visual appeal of native plant landscaping. This includes print, online, and social media platforms, as well as participation in local events and trade shows.

7. **Client Acquisition**: Seek out initial clients and establish long-term relationships by offering impeccable service and high-quality work. Obtain testimonials and positive reviews to build a robust reputation in the industry.

The growing demand for eco-friendly landscaping solutions and the increasing environmental consciousness of consumers make 2024 an ideal year to launch a native plant landscaping services start-up. By focusing on the ecological, aesthetic, and cost advantages of native plants and providing outstanding service, this business will attract a passionate client base and contribute to a greener, more sustainable future.

JAIME GEHLY

AI-Driven Climate Change Solutions

In recent years, the threat of climate change has become a major concern for governments, industries, and individuals worldwide. As the demand for sustainable and efficient solutions grows, an AI-driven climate change solutions start-up business has the potential to be highly successful in 2024. There are numerous reasons supporting this prospect, including a surge in climate change awareness, increased funding, advancements in AI technology, and cross-domain collaborations. In order to effectively establish and grow this start-up, a series of strategic steps must be executed, which will be outlined in this summary.

1. **Climate Change Awareness and Regulations**: Since the Paris Agreement's adoption in 2015, climate change awareness has skyrocketed, placing significant emphasis on adopting sustainable practices and limiting greenhouse gas emissions. In 2024, more stringent regulations and global targets remain key motivators for countries and industries, leading to increased receptiveness and adoption of AI-driven solutions that can mitigate climate change.

2. **Increased Funding Opportunities and Collaborations**: Governments, investors, and venture capitalists are increasingly recognizing the potential of AI-driven climate change solutions start-ups, leading to greater funding opportunities. Additionally, cross-domain collaborations between climate science specialists and AI experts will enable the creation of highly effective solutions, further driving the start-up's success.

3. **Advancements in AI Technology**: The continuous improvement in AI technology, including GPT-4 and subsequent iterations, allows for more accurate modeling, prediction, and optimization of climate change solutions. By leveraging advanced AI capabilities, the start-up will be uniquely positioned to offer innovative tools and platforms that tackle climate change challenges.

To Successfully Establish an AI-Driven Climate Change Solutions Start-Up in 2024, the Following Steps are Crucial:

1. **Identifying the Niche**: It is essential to define a specific niche within climate change that can benefit from AI-driven solutions. Examples include renewable energy optimization, agriculture, carbon capture, or climate modeling. This focus will enable the start-up to create higher quality and more targeted solutions.

2. **Assembling a Highly-Skilled Team**: Bringing together a group of talented individuals with expertise in various domains such as climate science, AI, data science, and software development is vital to develop state-of-the-art solutions.

3. **Developing and Validating the AI Solution**: Once a niche is defined and the team is assembled, the next step is to create an AI-driven solution tailored to address the particular climate change issue. This process involves data gathering, model development, and extensive validation of the solution to ensure its effectiveness and accuracy.

4. **Building a Network**: Developing strong relationships with key stakeholders, including government agencies, industry partners, and domain experts is crucial for business growth. Establishing trust with these stakeholders accelerates adoption and fosters potential collaborations.

5. **Securing Funding**: Pitch the start-up's value proposition and potential impact to investors and venture capitalists to secure financial backing. Additionally, keep an eye on relevant grants, local funding schemes, and other financing opportunities.

6. **Continuous Improvement**: After launching the AI-driven solution, it is essential to gather feedback, continuously iterate, and improve the product to ensure it remains effective, relevant, and competitive within the market.

In conclusion, driving the development of an AI-driven climate change solution start-up in 2024 promises substantial growth and success, demonstrated through a booming demand, advancements in AI technology, and increased funding opportunities. By thoroughly following the previously mentioned steps, it is possible to make a significant impact in the fight against climate change.

JAIME GEHLY

Smart Urban Farming Solutions

A smart urban farming solutions business will be poised for success due to factors such as population growth, increasing environmental concerns, evolving consumer demands, and technological advancements. By implementing data-driven, resource-efficient, and scalable farming techniques, a start-up in this field would be well-positioned to capitalize on these trends and contribute to the development of sustainable and resilient urban food systems.

The Following Basic Steps are Recommended for Launching a Successful Smart Urban Farming Start-up:

1. **Market Research**: Thoroughly research the urban farming industry to assess the competitive landscape, identify target customers, and determine the most viable business model. Factors to consider include market overview, growth factors, challenges, market segments, key players, and emerging trends.

2. **Formulate a Business Plan**: Develop a comprehensive business plan outlining the objectives, strategies, and business structure. Include market analysis, product offerings, financial projections, and a roadmap for short-term and long-term growth. This plan will serve as a guide for setting up and running the business and will be critical in securing financial support from investors or banks.

3. **Secure Funding**: Determine the level of financial investment required to establish and operate the start-up. Evaluate possible funding sources, such as bank loans, government grants, venture capital, angel investors, or crowdfunding platforms. Present a compelling case for investment, showcasing the market potential, skilled management team, and revenue projections.

4. **Choose the Right Technology**: Research and identify the most suitable technologies for the company, focusing on solutions that enable precision agriculture, efficient resource use, and maximum crop yield. Consider the use of IoT devices, artificial intelligence, machine learning, vertical farming, hydroponics, and aeroponics to optimize crop production and reduce the environmental footprint.

5. **Assemble a Skilled Team**: Hire a team of experienced professionals with expertise in agriculture, horticulture, engineering, data analysis, and marketing.

A diverse and qualified team will play a critical role in developing innovative products and strategies that drive the success of the start-up.

6. **Legal and Regulatory Compliance**: Determine and fulfill all legal and regulatory requirements, such as business registration, tax requirements, permits, licenses, and insurance coverage. Adherence to these regulations will ensure smooth operations and minimize the risk of penalties or setbacks.

7. **Develop and Maintain Strong Customer Relationships**: Establish long-term relationships with customers by offering customized smart urban farming solutions tailored to their specific needs. Focus on excellent customer service, timely delivery, and after-sales support to build trust and loyalty among clients.

8. **Continuous Learning and Adaptation**: As the industry evolves and new technologies emerge, engage in ongoing professional development and constantly refine business strategies. Stay up-to-date with the latest trends, technologies, and tools related to the smart urban farming sector to ensure the company remains competitive and relevant in the ever-changing landscape.

By following these basic steps, a smart urban farming start-up will be well-positioned for success in 2024 as the demand for sustainable, local, and efficient food production continues to grow. Embracing innovative technologies and strategies, such a start-up will not only contribute to improving food security but also play a pivotal role in addressing pressing environmental issues.

Ethical and Social Impact

AI-Based Talent Acquisition Platforms

The demand for rapid technological advances and skilled talent is on the rise, making the talent acquisition industry a promising sector for business growth. An AI-based talent acquisition start-up has the potential to be a lucrative venture in 2024 by maximizing efficiency, minimizing costs, and aiding companies in finding appropriate candidates for their open positions.

Market Potential:

1. **Growing Demand for Skilled Professionals**: Industries like technology, healthcare, finance, and digital marketing continue to grow, resulting in a higher need for qualified professionals across the globe.

2. **AI-Driven Automation**: The increasing use of AI in various industries reinforces the need for businesses to stay competitive and adopt AI-driven tools for tasks like recruitment and selection processes.

3. **The Impact of Remote Work**: Remote work has experienced a significant surge due to the pandemic, making it imperative for organizations to seek talent beyond geographical limitations.

Why AI-based Talent Acquisition Platforms Are Money Makers in 2024:

1. **Cost-Effectiveness**: AI-driven screening and selection tools ensure that companies save valuable resources by helping them identify suitable candidates faster and with minimal human intervention.

2. **Improved Efficiency**: AI algorithms can sort through large volumes of applications, analyze profiles, and shortlist candidates in a fraction of the time taken by traditional methods.

3. **Enhanced Candidate Experience**: AI-based platforms offer personalized, user-friendly experiences for candidates, boosting their satisfaction and the likelihood of them accepting job offers.

4. **Better Quality of Hires**: Through predictive analytics, AI systems can identify candidates who fit best with the company's culture and job requirements, improving employee productivity and retention rates.

5. **Competitive Edge**: Early adoption of AI-based talent acquisition platforms positions companies at the forefront of the industry, making them top choices for customers and investors alike.

Basic Steps to Start an AI-based Talent Acquisition Platforms Start-up:

1. **Market Research**: Thoroughly research the HR technology market to identify competition, gaps to fill, and potential customers.

2. **Develop a Unique Selling Proposition (USP)**: Define a specific niche and innovative solutions that will differentiate your AI-based platform from its competitors.

3. **Assemble a Skilled Team**: Form a diverse and talented team with expertise in AI, software development, HR, and business management to develop and maintain the platform.

4. **Design the Platform**: Design a user-friendly platform with powerful AI algorithms to handle tasks such as candidate sourcing, screening, and selection.

5. **Seek Funding**: Identify potential investors and explore funding options (angel investors, venture capital, crowdfunding) to secure the necessary capital for growth.

6. **Test and Iterate**: Launch a minimum viable product (MVP) to gather user feedback and make improvements before launching the final product.

7. **Develop Strategic Partnerships**: Collaborate with relevant industry players, like HR consultants, job boards, or recruitment agencies, to increase visibility and access to potential customers.

8. **Implement Marketing and Sales Strategies**: Spread awareness and drive adoption through targeted marketing campaigns, offering demos, and providing excellent customer support.

In conclusion, an AI-based talent acquisition platform has the potential to be a highly successful start-up in 2024 due to its efficiency, cost-effectiveness, and competitive edge. By following the outlined steps, entrepreneurs can seize this opportunity and carve their niche in the rapidly evolving talent acquisition industry.

JAIME GEHLY

Ethical AI Consultation and Implementation Services

In an increasingly digitized world where artificial intelligence solutions are transforming businesses and society, the need for ethical AI consultation and implementation is more important than ever. Rising awareness about the potential consequences of AI systems and the demand for robust ethical frameworks have created a unique opportunity for launching an ethical AI consultation and implementation start-up. The success of such a business venture rests on its ability to develop and implement customized ethical guidelines, deliver AI solutions responsibly, and maintain a proactive stance on evolving ethical standards. This document outlines the reasons behind the projected success of this start-up in 2024 and beyond, as well as the essential steps required to establish the business.

Key Reasons for Success:

1. **Growing Market Demand**: As AI technology continues to advance, it is expected that businesses across various sectors will invest further in AI solutions. This exponential growth will extend the demand for ethical AI consultation and implementation services to ensure fair, reliable, and accountable practices within the industry.

2. **Heightened Ethical Awareness**: High-profile concerns about bias, privacy, and transparency in AI have generated greater awareness of ethical AI issues. This increased interest presents an opportunity for a start-up that specializes in helping businesses establish ethical AI practices to succeed in the market.

3. **Governmental and Regulatory Pressure**: Governments and regulatory bodies are continuously proposing new guidelines for ethical AI development and deployment. A start-up that stays current with evolving policies and compliance requirements will be well-positioned to assist businesses in navigating these changing landscapes.

4. **Competitive Advantage**: Companies incorporating ethical AI practices will gain an edge in establishing trust both with customers and within the industry. This trust reflects positively on the start-up offering consultation and implementation services and contributes to its long-term success.

Basic Steps to Establish the Start-Up:

1. **Assess Market Feasibility**: Conduct thorough market research to determine potential customers, competition, and specific services in demand. This research will inform the start-up's approach to pricing and service offerings based on market conditions and consumer concerns.

2. **Develop a Business Plan**: A comprehensive business plan is crucial to the success of any start-up. This document should outline the company's mission, vision, and objectives, as well as address operational, financial, and marketing strategies.

3. **Assemble a Strong Team**: The start-up's team should consist of a diverse group of individuals with expertise in AI, ethics, legal and regulatory frameworks, and consulting. This combination of knowledge and expertise will allow the start-up to provide well-rounded, comprehensive services.

4. **Establish Partnerships**: Forge strategic alliances with AI technology companies, industry regulators, and other stakeholders to establish credibility and enable the sharing of best practices, resources, and support.

5. **Develop Ethical AI Guidelines**: Create a framework of ethical AI principles to guide the development and implementation of AI solutions. These guidelines should be adaptable and customizable to suit the unique needs and objectives of the business clientele.

6. **Launch Marketing and Sales Campaigns**: Raise awareness about the start-up's services through a combination of digital and traditional marketing channels, targeting potential customers that are currently investing in AI solutions or looking to expand their AI capabilities ethically.

In conclusion, the rapidly evolving AI landscape and the growing demand for ethical solutions make 2024 an opportune moment for launching an ethical AI consultation and implementation start-up business. By understanding market demand, keeping pace with regulatory changes, and embodying ethical AI practices, this start-up can lay the foundation for a sustainable, impactful business in the AI sector.

JAIME GEHLY

The Future Of IoT

JAIME GEHLY

A Success Story from the Lighting Industry

In this chapter, we will delve into the inspiring journey of an entrepreneur who successfully built a start-up in the Internet of Things (IoT) lighting industry. We will also discuss how this innovative company is bridging the gap between the physical world and the Metaverse, offering fresh insights for aspiring entrepreneurs.

Internet of Things (IoT) - The Building Block of Future Innovations:

IoT, or the Internet of Things, is an intricate network that connects billions of physical devices worldwide, allowing them to collect and share data. This technological revolution offers a new level of intelligence to objects that would otherwise be 'dumb', enabling real-time communication without human intervention. Whether it's a smart lightbulb that can be controlled via a smartphone app, a smart thermostat that adjusts office temperature, or a driverless truck that can navigate the roads autonomously, the IoT is transforming the fabric of our world, making it smarter and more responsive.

The Intersection of IoT and Lighting Industry:

In the realm of IoT, the lighting industry has seen a significant transformation. Traditional lighting solutions have been upgraded with smart features, bringing about a new era of IoT lighting. These smart lighting systems can be controlled remotely, offer energy conservation, and can even provide crucial data in real-time. The potential of IoT in the lighting industry is vast, and it presents lucrative opportunities for entrepreneurs.

The Journey of an IoT Lighting Company CEO:

CEO of Environments, Erin McDannald, has become a trailblazer in the IoT lighting industry. Her journey is a testament to the potential of IoT and a source of inspiration for aspiring entrepreneurs. Driven by the frustration of dealing with multiple incompatible systems and the need for a unifying platform, Erin and her team created Elevated Environments. This simple solution brings every element of your workplace, as well as the connectivity and vast possibilities of the Metaverse, together in one seamless app. Her vision was to create smart lights that not only provided illumination but also communicated valuable data, thereby making buildings 'smart.'

The Unique Features of IoT Lighting Products:

Environments' IoT lighting products are a step above traditional lighting solutions. The smart lights are capable of gathering valuable data like light levels, power consumption, diagnostics, and user preferences. This data is then projected into a digital twin, a virtual replica of the physical system, to create interactive environments for businesses.

Bridging the Gap between the Metaverse and Physical Reality:

Erin McDannald envisions IoT as a digital bridge, merging the physical and digital worlds seamlessly. Her company is working on integrating IoT lighting with the Metaverse, the virtual reality space where users can interact with a computer-based environment and other users.

"We have a patented system to build windows in our digital twins and put cameras on the analog side to seamlessly connect the two worlds."

This innovative integration presents numerous opportunities for businesses and consumers, from immersive UX/UI to spatial communication and interactive environments. This technology has the potential to greatly enhance many industries including education, healthcare, gaming, and more.

The Challenges and Triumphs in Developing Innovative Technology:

Developing innovative technology is not without its hurdles. One of the major challenges faced by McDannald was the lack of standardization in IoT integrations. Each sensor spoke its own language and had unique features.

"I had 17 widgets for my building controls and just wanted one. It started as a project for our firm to create one easy stack. It became so much more."

However, the company overcame this challenge by focusing on branding and data analytics, strategically choosing the sensors to integrate, and using the same data capture sources for every company on their system.

Leveraging Partnerships and Collaborations for Innovation:

Strategic partnerships and collaborations played a significant role in driving innovation at Environments. The company recently integrated with a prominent tech stack, reinforcing the importance of owning as many parts of the stack as possible and being strategic about integrations.

Impact of IoT Lighting Solutions on Businesses and Individuals:

Environments' IoT lighting solutions have made a significant impact on businesses, starting with their own company as the first proof of concept. Their IoT integration allows businesses to meter their buildings' energy and activity using the most powerful analytics currently available in the market. This allows for greener, more cost-efficient operations, as well as heightened security and 24/7 monitoring of environmental data in case of a malfunction or unexpected event. Through innovative thinking, Environments has used this data to create a virtual replica of the physical environment along with a unique and functional way to facilitate the interaction between these two worlds. The potential for integrating sensors to collect information and finding new and exciting ways to utilize such data is astounding and only time will tell how this technology will help to shape the future.

Words of Wisdom for Aspiring Entrepreneurs:

For aspiring entrepreneurs interested in starting an IoT-based start-up, Erin McDannald gives the following advice:

"Run lean, be ninja agile. Fail fast and learn from it. Pivot when needed. Let the market lead you. Think 8 chess moves down the board and reverse engineer."

Erin McDannald believes in giving people something to believe in and resonates with a quote by Douglas Rushkoff:

"It is not a matter of rejecting the digital or technological, it is a matter of retrieving the values we are in danger of leaving behind and then embedding them in the digital infrastructure."

As we move forward, the IoT industry will continue to evolve, offering exciting opportunities for entrepreneurs. With the right strategies and a clear vision, the next success story in the IoT lighting industry could be yours.

For more info on Erin McDannald and Environments visit:

www.Environments.tech
www.LightingEnvironments.com

101 BEST START-UP BUSINESS IDEAS FOR 2024 ACCORDING TO ADVANCED A.I.

www.ingramcontent.com/pod-product-compliance
Lightning Source LLC
Chambersburg PA
CBHW070421240526
45472CB00019B/87